HOW TO BUDGET AND MANAGE YOUR MONEY WISELY

A No-Nonsense Guide to Budgeting,
Saving, and Reaching Your Financial Goals

JORDAN MOTIVATOR

TABLE OF CONTENT

INTRODUCTION

Did you know that a staggering 78% of Americans live paycheck to paycheck, and 1 in 3 has no savings at all? It's a shocking reality that highlights the pervasive issue of poor money management. In a world where financial stability seems elusive for many, the importance of learning how to budget and manage money wisely cannot be overstated.

Financial struggles often stem from a lack of effective budgeting and money management. From mounting debt to the constant stress of living on the edge, the consequences of neglecting your financial health are far-reaching. Many find themselves caught in a cycle of paycheck dependency, unable to break free and achieve their financial goals.

But fear not, as there is a solution to these money woes. This guide is your compass to navigate the intricate landscape of personal finance, offering practical insights and strategies to empower you on your journey toward financial well-being.

In this book, we will explore:

Creating a Realistic Budget: Learn how to establish a budget that reflects your income, expenses, and financial goals. Discover various budgeting methods to find the one that suits your lifestyle.

Cutting Expenses: Uncover practical tips and tricks to trim unnecessary costs, allowing you to allocate more funds to your priorities and savings.

Getting Out of Debt: Understand the different types of debt and develop a personalized plan to conquer it. Explore consolidation and negotiation strategies to regain control of your finances.

Building Savings: Delve into the importance of saving money and explore strategies to build an emergency fund and save for future goals.

As you embark on this journey, remember that small changes in your financial habits can yield significant results. It's time to break free from the chains of financial stress and seize control of your money.

Keep reading to discover actionable steps that will help you start budgeting effectively, save more, and ultimately reach your financial goals. To kickstart your journey, we've included a complimentary budget template that you can download and use immediately. Your path to financial freedom begins here – let's get started!

Overview of the Importance of Budgeting

Overview of the Importance of Budgeting:

In the complex tapestry of personal finance, budgeting stands out as a fundamental and transformative thread that weaves together the fabric of financial well-being. At its essence, budgeting is not just about numbers on a spreadsheet; it's a strategic tool that empowers individuals to take control of their financial destinies.

Financial Clarity and Awareness:

Creating a budget gives you a broad perspective of your financial situation. By meticulously detailing your income, expenses, and financial goals, you gain a crystal-clear understanding of where your money comes from and where it goes. This awareness serves as the cornerstone for informed financial decision-making.

Goal Alignment and Prioritization:

A well-crafted budget acts as a compass, guiding you toward your financial objectives. It helps you identify and prioritize your goals, whether it's saving for a dream vacation, buying a home, or planning for retirement. With a budget, you can allocate resources efficiently, ensuring that your financial efforts align with your aspirations.

Expense Control and Resource Optimization:

Budgeting is a powerful tool for curbing unnecessary spending and maximizing the utility of your resources. By categorizing expenses and setting limits, you can identify areas where you may be overspending and redirect those funds toward more meaningful endeavors, such as savings or debt repayment.

Debt Prevention and Management:

Proactive budgeting acts as a shield against accumulating debt. By carefully managing your finances, you can avoid the pitfalls of living beyond your means and falling into the debt trap. For those already grappling with debt, a budget serves as a roadmap for repayment, offering a structured path toward financial freedom.

Emergency Preparedness:

Life is unpredictable, and financial emergencies can arise at any moment. A well-constructed budget includes provisions for an emergency fund, acting as a safety net during unforeseen circumstances. This financial cushion provides peace of mind and ensures that you're prepared to weather unexpected storms without derailing your long-term financial plans.

Stress Reduction and Financial Well-Being:

The mental and emotional impact of financial stress is undeniable. Budgeting alleviates this burden by instilling a sense of control and discipline. When you have a clear financial plan, you can navigate life's uncertainties with confidence, promoting overall well-being and peace of mind.

In essence, budgeting is the cornerstone of financial empowerment. It transforms financial chaos into order, uncertainty into security, and dreams into achievable goals. As we delve into the intricacies of budgeting, remember that this process is not a constraint but a liberating force, propelling you toward a future of financial prosperity and fulfillment.

The Benefits of Effective Money Management

Effective money management is akin to holding the reins of your financial destiny, steering it toward stability, security, and prosperity. Beyond the mere act of budgeting, proficient financial management yields a myriad of advantages that extend far beyond the realm of dollars and cents. Here are the key benefits of mastering the art of money management:

Financial Stability:

A well-structured financial plan fosters stability by ensuring that your income aligns with your expenses. This stability acts as a buffer against economic uncertainties, providing a solid foundation even during challenging times.

Goal Achievement:

Effective money management transforms aspirations into achievable goals. Whether it's buying a home, traveling the world, or retiring comfortably, a strategic financial plan helps you allocate resources toward your objectives, turning dreams into tangible realities.

Debt Reduction and Prevention:

Skillful money management enables you to proactively address and eliminate debt. By creating a budget that prioritizes debt repayment, you can break free from the shackles of financial burden and work toward a debt-free future.

Improved Credit Score:

Responsible money management positively impacts your credit score. Timely bill payments, debt management, and a balanced credit utilization ratio contribute to a healthy credit profile, opening doors to better interest rates and financial opportunities.

Increased Savings:

Budgeting allows you to systematically save for short-term goals, emergencies, and long-term investments. The habit of saving not only provides a financial safety net but also facilitates wealth-building and financial independence.

Reduced Stress and Anxiety:

A clear financial plan reduces the stress associated with money-related uncertainties. Knowing where your money goes and having the tools to manage it effectively promotes peace of mind and mental well-being.

Enhanced Decision-Making:

Money management equips you with the information needed to make informed financial decisions. From investments to major purchases, having a comprehensive understanding of your financial situation empowers you to make choices aligned with your long-term objectives.

Flexibility and Adaptability:

Life is dynamic, and financial circumstances can change. Effective money management fosters adaptability, allowing you to adjust your financial plan in response to evolving goals, unexpected expenses, or shifts in income.

Financial Independence:

Mastering money management is a crucial step toward achieving financial independence. By taking control of your finances, you reduce reliance on external sources and pave the way for greater autonomy over your economic future.

Generational Wealth Building:

Effective money management transcends personal benefits, creating a legacy of financial literacy and stability for future generations. Sound financial practices can be passed down, fostering a cycle of prosperity within families.

In essence, the benefits of effective money management extend far beyond immediate financial gains. It is a holistic approach that not only safeguards your present but also lays the groundwork for a secure and prosperous future. As you embark on the journey of mastering your finances, recognize that the dividends of disciplined money management are not just monetary – they enrich every aspect of your life.

Chapter 1: Setting Financial Goals

Short-Term, Mid-Term, And Long-Term Goals

Setting goals is a fundamental aspect of personal and financial planning, providing a roadmap to guide your efforts and aspirations. Goals are typically categorized into short-term, mid-term, and long-term, each serving a unique purpose in shaping your financial journey.

Short-Term Goals:

Definition: Short-term goals typically span from a few days to a couple of years and are focused on immediate needs or desires.

Examples:

Building an emergency fund

Paying off a small debt

Saving for a vacation

Purchasing a new electronic device

Covering an unexpected medical expense

Characteristics:

Achievable in a relatively short time frame

Typically involves smaller financial commitments

Provides a sense of accomplishment and motivation

Helps establish the habit of setting and achieving goals

Mid-Term Goals:

Definition: Mid-term goals typically cover a time frame of two to five years, striking a balance between short-term immediacy and long-term vision.

Examples:

Saving for a down payment on a home

Completing a certification or degree program

Paying off a car loan

Starting a small business

Saving for a major home renovation

Characteristics:

Require a moderate level of financial commitment and planning

Often involve significant life events or milestones

May contribute to long-term objectives or serve as stepping stones

Long-Term Goals:

Definition: Long-term goals typically span beyond five years and are focused on substantial achievements and life-changing events.

Examples:

Saving for retirement

Paying off a mortgage

Funding a child's education

Achieving financial independence

Establishing a charitable foundation

Characteristics:

Require sustained commitment and discipline

Often involve substantial financial resources

Shape the overarching direction of one's life and financial plans

May necessitate adjustments and fine-tuning over time

Considerations:

Hierarchy and Interconnectedness: Short-term goals often lay the foundation for mid-term goals, which, in turn, contribute to the achievement of long-term goals.

Flexibility: Life is dynamic, and circumstances change. It's essential to periodically review and adjust your goals based on evolving priorities, financial status, and external factors.

SMART Criteria: Whether short-term, mid-term, or long-term, effective goals are Specific, Measurable, Achievable, Relevant, and Time-bound.

Setting and pursuing goals across these time frames allows you to balance immediate needs with future aspirations, ensuring a holistic and purposeful approach to your personal and financial growth.

Planning for expenses vs. Wants

One of the crucial aspects of effective financial management is distinguishing between essential expenses and discretionary wants. Successfully navigating this distinction allows individuals to prioritize spending, allocate resources wisely, and work towards financial goals. Here's a closer look at planning for expenses versus wants:

Essential Expenses:

Definition: Essential expenses are necessary costs that are fundamental to maintaining a basic standard of living. These typically include items and services vital for survival, well-being, and fulfilling responsibilities.

Examples:

Housing (rent or mortgage)

Utilities (electricity, water, gas)

Groceries and essential food items

Health insurance and medical expenses

Transportation (commuting, vehicle maintenance)

Planning Considerations:

Non-Negotiable: Essential expenses are often non-negotiable; they must be paid to ensure basic needs are met.

Priority: These expenses take precedence over discretionary spending and should be accounted for in your budget before allocating funds to other categories.

Consistency: Many essential expenses are recurring and require consistent planning to avoid financial strain.

Discretionary Wants:

Definition: Discretionary wants encompass non-essential or optional expenditures that enhance lifestyle but are not critical for day-to-day survival.

Examples:

Dining out or entertainment

Non-essential clothing and accessories

Hobbies and leisure activities

Luxury or non-essential technology upgrades

Vacations and travel

Planning Considerations:

Variable Nature: Discretionary wants often vary in terms of timing and magnitude, providing flexibility in spending decisions.

Budget Allocation: Allocate funds for discretionary wants after addressing essential expenses and saving for financial goals.

Prioritization: Evaluate the importance of discretionary wants relative to your overall financial objectives.

Strategies for Effective Planning:

Budgeting: Create a comprehensive budget that clearly outlines both essential expenses and discretionary wants. This helps in managing income and allocating funds intentionally.

Prioritization: Prioritize essential expenses to ensure the most critical needs are met before allocating funds to non-essential wants.

Emergency Fund: Establishing an emergency fund helps cover unexpected essential expenses, reducing the risk of financial strain during unforeseen circumstances.

Goal Alignment: Align spending decisions with your financial goals. Assess whether a discretionary want aligns with your long-term objectives before making the purchase.

Balancing Act:

Flexibility: While essential expenses are typically fixed, discretionary wants offer flexibility. Adjust spending based on your financial situation and goals.

Mindful Spending: Regularly evaluate your spending habits to ensure they align with your priorities. Be mindful of impulse purchases that may divert funds from essential needs.

By consciously planning for both essential expenses and discretionary wants, individuals can strike a balance that promotes financial stability, goal achievement, and overall well-being. It's the art of navigating the fine line between needs and desires, ensuring financial decisions align with one's broader objectives.

Lifestyle factors to consider

Your lifestyle plays a significant role in shaping your financial landscape. Understanding and accounting for lifestyle factors is crucial for effective financial planning and decision-making. Here are important lifestyle elements to think about:

Income and Earning Potential:

Current Income: Assess your current income, including salary, bonuses, and other sources of earnings.

Earning Potential: Consider your career trajectory, skills development, and potential for increased income over time.

Expenses and Spending Habits:

Fixed vs. Variable Expenses: Differentiate between fixed monthly expenses (rent, utilities) and variable expenses (entertainment, dining out).

Lifestyle Inflation: Be aware of the tendency for expenses to rise with increased income and adjust spending accordingly.

Debt Obligations:

Type and Amount of Debt: Identify and categorize your debts, including credit cards, student loans, and mortgages.

Debt Repayment Plan: Develop a strategy for managing and repaying debts, considering interest rates and financial goals.

Savings and Emergency Fund:

Savings Goals: Define short-term and long-term savings goals, such as an emergency fund, travel fund, or retirement savings.

Emergency Fund: Ensure you have a financial cushion to cover unexpected expenses without disrupting your lifestyle.

Career and Job Stability:

Job Security: Assess the stability of your current job and industry trends.

Career Aspirations: Consider the potential for career advancement and whether it aligns with your lifestyle goals.

Family and Dependents:

Family Size: Evaluate the financial impact of your family size on housing, education, and other expenses.

Dependent Care: Consider costs associated with childcare, education, and other dependent-related expenses.

Health and Wellness:

Healthcare Costs: Factor in routine healthcare expenses and potential medical emergencies.

Wellness Investments: Budget for fitness, nutrition, and other wellness-related expenditures.

Housing Choices:

Rent vs. Own: Assess the financial implications of renting versus owning a home.

Location: Consider the cost of living in different locations and how it aligns with your lifestyle preferences.

Travel and Leisure:

Vacation Budget: Plan for travel expenses and set a budget for leisure activities.

Entertainment Choices: Evaluate the financial impact of your entertainment choices, such as dining out, hobbies, and recreational activities.

Financial Goals and Aspirations:

Short-Term and Long-Term Goals: Define your financial goals, including buying a home, saving for education, and planning for retirement.

Investment Strategy: Align your investment strategy with your risk tolerance and long-term financial objectives.

Technology and Lifestyle Tools:

Tech Expenses: Consider the costs associated with technology, including gadgets, subscriptions, and digital services.

Budgeting Apps: Utilize budgeting apps and financial tools to streamline and enhance your money management.

Social and Networking Activities:

Social Spending: Be mindful of expenses related to socializing, events, and networking activities.

Balancing Social and Financial Priorities: Strike a balance between maintaining social connections and adhering to your financial goals.

By taking these lifestyle factors into account, you can tailor your financial plan to align with your unique circumstances and aspirations. A holistic approach that considers both your present lifestyle and future goals is key to achieving financial well-being.

Importance Of Goal Setting

Goal setting is not just a theoretical exercise but a dynamic and transformative process that underpins personal and professional growth. Whether in the realm of finances, career, education, or personal development, setting and pursuing goals is a fundamental practice with numerous benefits. Here's a closer look at the importance of goal setting:

Clarity of Purpose:

Defining Direction: Goal setting provides a clear roadmap, helping individuals define their purpose and direction in life.

Focused Energy: It concentrates energy and efforts toward specific objectives, preventing aimless pursuits and distractions.

Motivation and Commitment:

Intrinsic Motivation: Goals serve as powerful motivators, tapping into intrinsic desires and aspirations.

Sustained Commitment: Clearly defined goals foster commitment, keeping individuals focused on their objectives even during challenges.

Measurable Progress:

Tracking Success: Goals offer measurable milestones, enabling individuals to track and celebrate their progress.

Identifying Challenges: Setbacks become opportunities for learning and improvement, contributing to overall development.

Time Management:

Prioritizing Activities: Goal setting facilitates effective time management by helping individuals prioritize activities aligned with their objectives.

Minimizing Procrastination: Clear goals reduce procrastination, encouraging timely action and accomplishment.

Enhanced Decision-Making:

Aligned Choices: Goals act as a filter for decision-making, guiding individuals to make choices aligned with their long-term objectives.

Reduced Ambiguity: Clarity in goals reduces ambiguity, aiding in confident decision-making.

Personal Development:

Continuous Learning: Pursuing goals often involves acquiring new skills and knowledge, fostering continuous personal development.

Resilience and Adaptability: Overcoming challenges in goal pursuit builds resilience and adaptability, valuable attributes in various aspects of life.

Improved Focus and Efficiency:

Focused Efforts: Goal setting hones focus, preventing dispersion of energy across too many pursuits.

Increased Efficiency: A well-defined goal enhances efficiency, as efforts are directed toward achieving specific outcomes.

Enhanced Self-Esteem:

Sense of Achievement: Accomplishing goals boosts self-esteem and confidence.

Positive Reinforcement: Celebrating small victories reinforces a positive mindset, contributing to overall well-being.

Long-Term Vision:

Building a Future: Goals create a long-term vision, helping individuals shape their desired futures.

Sustainability: Sustainable goals contribute to a sense of purpose and fulfillment over the course of a lifetime.

Balanced Life:

Holistic Approach: Goal setting encourages a balanced approach to life, considering various aspects such as career, relationships, health, and personal interests.

Preventing Burnout: Balancing goals helps avoid burnout by promoting a harmonious and sustainable lifestyle.

In essence, goal setting is a dynamic process that goes beyond mere achievement; it is a journey of self-discovery, growth, and fulfillment. By setting clear goals and committing to their pursuit, individuals unlock their potential and chart a course toward a more purposeful and satisfying life.

Chapter 2: Creating a Budget

Types Of Budgets (Zero-Based, 50/30/20, Etc.)

Budgeting is a fundamental aspect of personal finance that empowers individuals to manage their money effectively. Various budgeting methods cater to different financial goals, lifestyles, and preferences. Here are some popular types of budgets, each with its unique approach:

Zero-Based Budget:

Definition: In a zero-based budget, every dollar is assigned a specific purpose. The goal is for income minus expenses to equal zero, meaning that every dollar is allocated to spending, saving, or debt repayment.

Process: Categories are assigned a set amount, and adjustments are made until the budget balances at zero.

Benefits: Promotes detailed tracking of spending, ensures all income is allocated, and encourages intentional financial decisions.

50/30/20 Budget:

Rule of Thumb: This budgeting approach allocates 50% of income to needs, 30% to wants, and 20% to savings and debt repayment.

Needs: Essential expenses like housing, utilities, and groceries fall under the 50% category.

Wants: Non-essential spending, such as dining out or entertainment, is limited to 30%.

Savings/Debt Repayment: The remaining 20% is dedicated to building savings and paying down debt.

Envelope System:

Physical Allocation: In the envelope system, cash is divided into envelopes earmarked for specific spending categories.

Strict Limitations: Once an envelope is empty, spending in that category must cease until the next budgeting period.

Benefits: Promotes discipline, prevents overspending, and offers a tangible way to manage money.

Reverse Budget:

Savings-First Approach: The reverse budget focuses on saving a predetermined amount first before allocating the rest to expenses.

Prioritizing Goals: Savings goals are given top priority, ensuring that financial objectives are met before discretionary spending.

Benefits: Emphasizes the importance of saving and encourages a more intentional approach to spending.

80/20 Budget:

Savings Emphasis: This budget allocates 80% of income to living expenses and discretionary spending, while the remaining 20% is dedicated to savings and debt repayment.

Flexible Spending: Provides flexibility for personal spending preferences while still prioritizing savings.

Pay Yourself First:

Principle: In this approach, a predetermined portion of income is automatically directed towards savings or investments before any other expenses are considered.

Automated Transfers: Utilizes automatic transfers to prioritize savings goals and ensure consistency.

Benefits: Encourages a consistent savings habit and makes savings a non-negotiable part of the budget.

Line Item Budget:

Detailed Breakdown: A line item budget involves creating a detailed list of all income and expenses, assigning specific amounts to each category.

Thorough Tracking: Enables meticulous tracking of spending, making it easier to identify areas for adjustment.

Benefits: Offers a comprehensive view of where money is going and facilitates detailed financial planning.

Choosing the Right Budget:

Personalization: The effectiveness of a budget depends on personal preferences, financial goals, and lifestyle.

Trial and Error: It may take some experimentation to find the budgeting method that best suits individual needs.

Flexibility: A successful budget is one that can adapt to changing circumstances and priorities.

Ultimately, the key to successful budgeting is finding an approach that aligns with your financial goals and lifestyle, allowing you to manage your money in a way that promotes financial health and well-being.

Calculating Income And Expenses

Understanding your income and expenses is the cornerstone of effective financial management. By accurately assessing your financial inflows and outflows, you gain valuable insights that form the basis of informed decision-making and successful budgeting. Here's a guide on how to calculate your income and expenses:

Calculating Income

Employment Income:

Sum up your salary or hourly wages. Include any additional income sources, such as bonuses or overtime pay.

Consider other benefits like health insurance contributions or retirement plan contributions if they contribute to your overall compensation.

Self-Employment Income:

Add up all earnings from your business or freelance activities.

Account for variations in income, especially if your earnings fluctuate monthly.

Investment Income:

Include interest, dividends, and capital gains from investments.

Consider income generated from rental properties or any other investments.

Side Hustle or Gig Income:

If you have a side hustle or participate in gig work, calculate the income generated.

Include earnings from freelance work, consulting, or part-time jobs.

Government Benefits:

Include any government assistance or benefits you receive, such as social security, unemployment benefits, or disability payments.

Other Sources:

Account for any additional sources of income, such as alimony, child support, or gifts.

Calculating Expenses

Fixed Monthly Expenses:

Identify and list all fixed monthly expenses, including rent or mortgage, utilities, insurance premiums, and loan payments.

These are consistent, recurring costs that remain relatively stable each month.

Variable Monthly Expenses:

Record variable expenses that may fluctuate from month to month, such as groceries, dining out, entertainment, and transportation.

Use averages if specific amounts vary significantly.

Debt Repayment:

Include monthly payments for credit cards, student loans, and any other outstanding debts.

Note interest rates and terms for each debt.

Savings Contributions:

Deduct the amount you intend to save each month.

Include contributions to emergency funds, retirement accounts, or other savings goals.

Irregular Expenses:

Identify occasional or irregular expenses, such as annual insurance premiums, property taxes, or vehicle maintenance.

Divide these expenses by 12 to incorporate them into your monthly budget.

Miscellaneous and Discretionary Spending:

Account for discretionary spending on non-essential items like hobbies, subscriptions, or impulse purchases.

Be honest about your spending habits to ensure accuracy.

Net Income and Budgeting:

Calculate Net Income:

Take your entire monthly revenue and subtract it from your complete monthly spending.

The resulting amount is your net income, representing the money available for discretionary spending, savings, and debt repayment.

Adjust and Prioritize:

Make sure your budget is in line with your financial objectives by reviewing it.

If necessary, make adjustments to prioritize savings, reduce discretionary spending, or allocate funds to specific financial objectives.

Consistency and Monitoring:

Regularly track your income and expenses to ensure consistency.

Periodically review and update your budget as your financial situation evolves.

By diligently calculating your income and expenses, you gain a comprehensive understanding of your financial landscape. This knowledge empowers you to make informed decisions, set realistic financial goals, and cultivate healthy financial habits.

Recommended Budget Percentages

Setting budget percentages is a practical approach to allocate your income effectively and ensure a balanced financial life. While individual circumstances vary, these recommended budget percentages provide general guidelines to help you structure your spending, saving, and investing. Keep in mind that these are flexible recommendations, and adjustments may be necessary based on your unique financial goals and lifestyle.

Housing: 25-35%:

Include rent or mortgage payments, property taxes, homeowners or renters insurance, and utility bills.

Aim to keep housing costs within 25-35% of your gross income.

Transportation: 10-15%:

Account for car payments, fuel, insurance, maintenance, and public transportation costs.

Aim to spend no more than 10-15% of your income on transportation.

Groceries and Dining: 10-15%:

Include expenses related to groceries, dining out, and food delivery services.

Aim to allocate 10-15% of your income to food-related expenses.

Debt Repayment: 10-15%:

Cover payments for credit cards, student loans, personal loans, and other debts.

Aim to allocate 10-15% of your income to debt repayment.

Savings: 15-20%:

Prioritize savings, including contributions to emergency funds, retirement accounts, and other savings goals.

Aim to save 15-20% of your income.

Utilities and Bills: 5-10%:

Include expenses for utilities, phone bills, internet, and other monthly subscriptions.

Aim to keep utility and bill costs within 5-10% of your income.

Healthcare: 5-10%:

Cover health insurance premiums, co-pays, and other medical expenses.

Aim to allocate 5-10% of your income to healthcare costs.

Entertainment: 5-10%:

Include spending on hobbies, leisure activities, streaming services, and entertainment.

Aim to keep entertainment expenses within 5-10% of your income.

Personal Care and Clothing: 5-10%:

Account for expenses related to personal care products, clothing, and accessories.

Aim to spend 5-10% of your income on personal care and clothing.

Education and Training: 1-5%:

- Include costs for education, professional development, and training programs.

- Aim to allocate 1-5% of your income to education and training.

Miscellaneous: 5-10%:

- Cover miscellaneous expenses that may not fit into specific categories.

- Aim to keep miscellaneous spending within 5-10% of your income.

Charitable Giving: 1-5%:

- If charitable giving is a priority, allocate a percentage of your income for donations.

- Aim to give 1-5% of your income to charitable causes.

Investments: 5-15%:

- Include contributions to investment accounts such as stocks, bonds, and other investment vehicles.

- Aim to allocate 5-15% of your income to investments.

Adjusting Budget Percentages:

Flexibility: While these percentages offer a starting point, they are not rigid rules. Adjust based on your priorities, goals, and cost of living.

Changing Circumstances: Life circumstances may change, necessitating adjustments to your budget percentages.

Periodic Review: Regularly review and update your budget percentages to ensure alignment with your financial objectives.

By using these recommended budget percentages as a guide, you can create a balanced and sustainable financial plan that aligns with your goals and values. Keep in mind that personalization is key, and your budget should reflect your unique financial situation and aspirations.

Sample Budgets For Different Incomes

Creating a budget tailored to your income is a crucial step in managing your finances effectively. Below are sample budgets for different income levels to provide a general framework. Remember, these are just examples, and you should customize your budget based on your unique circumstances, priorities, and financial goals.

Sample Budget for Lower Income (e.g., $30,000 per year):

Income:

Monthly: $2,500

Budget Breakdown:

Housing (30%): $750

Rent or mortgage payment

Utilities

Transportation (15%): $375

Public transportation or fuel

Maintenance and insurance

Groceries and Dining (15%): $375

Groceries

Occasional dining out

Debt Repayment (10%): $250

Credit cards, student loans, etc.

Savings (10%): $250

Emergency fund

Small savings goals

Utilities and Bills (5%): $125

Phone bills, internet, subscriptions

Healthcare (5%): $125

Health insurance, co-pays

Entertainment (5%): $125

Hobbies, streaming services

Personal Care and Clothing (5%): $125

Personal care items, clothing

Miscellaneous (5%): $125

Unforeseen expenses

Sample Budget for Middle Income (e.g., $60,000 per year):

Income:

Monthly: $5,000

Budget Breakdown:

Housing (25%): $1,250

Rent or mortgage payment

Utilities

Transportation (15%): $750

Car expenses, fuel, insurance

Groceries and Dining (10%): $500

Groceries

Dining out

Debt Repayment (10%): $500

Credit cards, loans

Savings (15%): $750

Emergency fund

Retirement savings

Utilities and Bills (5%): $250

Phone bills, internet, subscriptions

Healthcare (5%): $250

Health insurance, medical costs

Entertainment (5%): $250

Hobbies, streaming services

Personal Care and Clothing (5%): $250

Personal care items, clothing

Miscellaneous (5%): $250

Unforeseen expenses

Sample Budget for Higher Income (e.g., $100,000 per year):

Income:

Monthly: $8,333

Budget Breakdown:

Housing (20%): $1,667

Mortgage payment or rent

Utilities, home maintenance

Transportation (10%): $833

Car expenses, fuel, insurance

Groceries and Dining (8%): $667

Groceries

Fine dining, entertainment

Debt Repayment (5%): $417

Credit cards, loans

Savings (20%): $1,667

Emergency fund

Retirement savings, investments

Utilities and Bills (4%): $333

Phone bills, internet, subscriptions

Healthcare (5%): $417

Health insurance, medical costs

Entertainment (7%): $583

Hobbies, travel, premium subscriptions

Personal Care and Clothing (5%): $417

Personal care items, clothing

Miscellaneous (6%): $500

Unforeseen expenses, luxury purchases

Adjust these sample budgets based on your specific needs, lifestyle, and financial goals. Regularly review and update your budget to ensure it reflects changes in your income, expenses, and priorities.

Budgeting Tools And Apps

Budgeting Tools and Apps: Navigating Your Financial Journey

In the digital age, managing your finances has become more accessible and efficient, thanks to a plethora of budgeting tools and apps designed to streamline the budgeting process, track spending, and enhance overall financial awareness. Here's a look at some popular budgeting tools and apps that can help you take control of your financial journey:

Mint:

Key Features:

Automatic categorization of transactions

Customizable budgeting goals

Credit score tracking

Bill payment reminders

Why Use It:

Comprehensive overview of your financial picture

Easy tracking of expenses and income

YNAB (You Need A Budget):

Key Features:

Rule-based budgeting system

Goal tracking and debt payoff tools

Real-time synchronization across devices

Educational resources on budgeting

Why Use It:

Focuses on giving every dollar a job

Encourages proactive budgeting and financial planning

Personal Capital:

Key Features:

Investment tracking and portfolio analysis

Retirement planning tools

Net worth calculation

Cash flow analysis

Why Use It:

Holistic approach to financial management

Ideal for those with investments and retirement goals

PocketGuard:

Key Features:

Automatic expense tracking

Budget tracking in real-time

Bill reminders and alerts

Savings goals tracking

Why Use It:

Quick and simple overview of your budget

Helps identify areas for potential savings

Wally:

Key Features:

Expense tracking with location-based services

Budgeting and savings goals

Receipt scanning for expense documentation

Why Use It:

User-friendly interface

Ideal for tracking daily expenses on the go

GoodBudget:

Key Features:

Envelope budgeting system

Shared budgets for families or couples

Expense tracking and reports

Why Use It:

Encourages mindful spending through envelope system

Collaborative budgeting for households

EveryDollar:

Key Features:

Zero-based budgeting approach

Customizable budget categories

Transaction tracking

Why Use It:

Aligns with the principles of Dave Ramsey's Financial Peace University

Simple and intuitive interface

Clarity Money:

Key Features:

Expense tracking and categorization

Bill negotiation service

Subscription tracking and cancellation assistance

Why Use It:

Focuses on improving financial health

Helps eliminate unnecessary subscriptions and bills

Honeydue:

Key Features:

Joint budgeting for couples

Bill tracking and reminders

Shared expense tracking

Why Use It:

Facilitates transparent financial communication between partners

Ideal for managing shared expenses and financial goals

Expensify:

Key Features:

Expense tracking and receipt scanning

Business expense reporting

Integrations with accounting software

Why Use It:

Ideal for business-related expense management

Streamlines the expense reporting process

Tips for Choosing a Budgeting Tool or App:

Compatibility: Ensure the tool is compatible with your devices (iOS, Android, web).

Security: Look for apps with robust security features to protect your financial data.

Ease of Use: Choose an app with an interface that suits your preferences and is easy to navigate.

Features: Consider the features offered and whether they align with your specific budgeting needs.

Integration: If you use other financial tools or services, check if the app integrates with them for a seamless experience.

Whichever tool or app you choose, the key is to find one that aligns with your financial goals, helps you stay organized, and empowers you to make informed financial decisions. Experiment with different tools until you find the one that best suits your needs and preferences.

Chapter 3: Reducing Expenses

Big Expense Areas To Cut Back On

Identifying and cutting back on big expense areas is a strategic approach to improving your financial health and achieving your savings goals. Here are some significant expense areas where you may find opportunities to reduce costs:

Housing Costs:

Rent or Mortgage: Consider downsizing or relocating to a more affordable area.

Utilities: Evaluate energy usage, explore more cost-effective providers, and invest in energy-efficient appliances.

Transportation:

Car Expenses: Assess whether owning a car is necessary. If possible, consider public transportation, carpooling, or ridesharing.

Insurance: Shop around for competitive insurance rates and consider increasing deductibles to lower premiums.

Food and Dining Out:

Groceries: Plan meals, buy in bulk, and look for discounts to cut grocery costs.

Dining Out: Limit restaurant visits, and consider cooking at home or opting for more budget-friendly eateries.

Subscription Services:

Streaming Services: Evaluate the necessity of multiple streaming subscriptions and consider eliminating redundant services.

Magazines and Subscriptions: Reevaluate the value of subscriptions, magazines, and memberships.

Entertainment and Leisure:

Concerts and Events: Choose less expensive events or limit attendance to special occasions.

Recreational Activities: Seek free or low-cost alternatives for hobbies and leisure activities.

Health and Wellness:

Gym Memberships: Explore budget-friendly fitness options, outdoor activities, or at-home workouts.

Unused Subscriptions: Cancel subscriptions for services or products that are not actively used.

Travel Expenses:

Vacations: Opt for budget-friendly destinations or consider alternatives like staycations.

Airfare: Be flexible with travel dates and explore discounts or travel rewards.

Debt Interest Payments:

Credit Cards: Negotiate lower interest rates, consolidate debt, or explore balance transfer options.

Loans: Refinance high-interest loans to lower monthly payments.

Shopping and Impulse Purchases:

Impulse Buying: Adopt a more mindful approach to shopping by creating a list and sticking to it.

Branded Products: Consider generic or less expensive alternatives for everyday items.

Technology and Electronics:

Gadgets: Evaluate the necessity of frequent technology upgrades and consider purchasing refurbished or older models.

Data Plans: Explore more cost-effective data plans for your devices.

Insurance Costs:

Health Insurance: Review health insurance plans for better coverage at a lower cost.

Life Insurance: Compare rates and consider adjusting coverage based on current needs.

Utilities and Bills:

Cable and Internet: Explore alternatives like streaming services or negotiate a better deal with your current provider.

Phone Plans: Switch to a more budget-friendly phone plan.

Childcare and Education:

Childcare Costs: Explore more affordable childcare options or consider sharing responsibilities with family members.

Education Expenses: Seek financial aid options, scholarships, or lower-cost educational alternatives.

Personal Care and Beauty:

Salon Visits: Stretch the time between salon visits or explore more affordable options.

Beauty Products: Look for budget-friendly alternatives and limit unnecessary purchases.

Bank and Credit Card Fees:

ATM Fees: Use in-network ATMs to avoid fees.

Credit Card Fees: Choose credit cards with lower or no annual fees.

Tips for Successful Cost Cutting:

Prioritize: Identify which expenses have the most significant impact on your budget and prioritize those for reduction.

Negotiate: Negotiate bills, interest rates, and insurance premiums to secure better deals.

Track Spending: Use budgeting tools to monitor spending habits and identify areas for improvement.

Set Goals: Clearly define your financial goals and allocate the savings from cost-cutting toward those objectives.

Regular Review: Periodically reassess your budget and spending to ensure continued financial discipline.

By targeting these significant expense areas, you can create more room in your budget for savings, debt repayment, and achieving your long-term financial goals. Adjustments may take time, but with consistency and dedication, you can make meaningful progress toward financial well-being.

Finding little ways to save daily

In the pursuit of financial wellness, small daily savings can accumulate into significant amounts over time. By adopting mindful spending habits and making subtle changes in your daily routines, you can boost your savings without drastically altering your lifestyle. Here are some practical tips to find little ways to save money every day:

Brown Bag It:

Daily Lunch: Prepare and bring your lunch to work instead of eating out. This not only saves money but can also be healthier.

Coffee at Home:

Beverages: Brew your coffee at home and carry it in a reusable cup to avoid daily coffee shop expenses.

Meal Planning:

Grocery Shopping: Plan your meals for the week, create a shopping list, and stick to it . By doing this, food waste is decreased and needless purchases are avoided.

Energy Conservation:

Unplug Devices: Unplug chargers and electronic devices when not in use to save on electricity costs.

Energy-Efficient Bulbs: Replace traditional light bulbs with energy-efficient ones.

Couponing and Discounts:

Online Shopping: Look for online coupons and discounts before making any purchase. Various browser extensions can help you find the best deals.

Public Transportation or Carpooling:

Daily Commute: If feasible, use public transportation or carpool to save on fuel and parking expenses.

DIY Snacks:

Snack Prep: Instead of buying expensive snacks, prepare your own at home. This is often healthier and more cost-effective.

Cancel Unnecessary Subscriptions:

Subscription Audits: Regularly review your subscriptions and cancel those you no longer use or need.

Water over Beverages:

Drinks: Opt for water instead of buying beverages when dining out. Not only is it healthier, but it's also often free.

Buy Generic Brands:

Groceries and Products: Consider purchasing generic or store-brand items instead of premium brands to save on costs without sacrificing quality.

Reusable Containers:

Takeout: Carry reusable containers for leftovers when dining out to avoid paying for takeaway boxes.

Library Usage:

Books and Movies: Instead of purchasing books or movies, use your local library to borrow them for free.

DIY Home Repairs:

Basic Fixes: Learn to handle minor home repairs and maintenance tasks instead of hiring professionals for every issue.

Free Fitness:

Exercise: Utilize free workout videos online or take advantage of community fitness classes.

Automate Savings:

Automatic Transfers: Set up automatic transfers to your savings account on payday to ensure consistent savings.

Track Monthly Subscriptions:

Review Monthly Bills: Periodically review your bank and credit card statements to identify and cancel unused subscriptions.

Homemade Cleaning Products:

Cleaning Supplies: Create your own cleaning products using simple ingredients, reducing the need to purchase expensive cleaners.

Shop Secondhand:

Clothing and Furniture: Explore thrift stores or online platforms for secondhand clothing, furniture, and other items.

Bulk Purchases:

Non-Perishables: Buy non-perishable items in bulk to take advantage of discounts and reduce the frequency of shopping trips.

Cashback Rewards:

Credit Card Rewards: Use credit cards that offer cashback or rewards programs for your regular purchases.

Tips for Success:

Start Small: Implement one or two changes at a time to avoid feeling overwhelmed.

Track Expenses: Regularly track your daily expenses using budgeting apps to identify areas for improvement.

Set Goals: Define short-term and long-term savings goals to stay motivated.

Celebrate Progress: Acknowledge and celebrate the small victories in your daily savings journey.

Remember, the key to finding little ways to save daily is consistency and a willingness to make small adjustments. Over time, these daily savings habits can have a significant impact on your overall financial well-being.

Negotiating Bills And Services

Negotiating bills and services is a powerful skill that can significantly impact your monthly expenses and contribute to long-term financial savings. Whether it's your utility bills, insurance premiums, or subscription services, taking the initiative to negotiate can lead to more favorable terms. The following is a step-by-step tutorial to assist you in negotiating:

Research and Understand the Market:

Knowledge is Power: Before negotiating, research the standard rates and terms for the service you're interested in. Knowing the market value strengthens your negotiating position.

Review Your Current Plan:

Understand Your Usage: Assess your usage patterns and needs to identify areas where you can potentially cut costs without sacrificing essential services.

Prepare and Plan Your Strategy:

Clarify Your Objectives: Clearly define what you want to achieve through negotiation—whether it's a lower monthly fee, better terms, or additional services.

Highlight Loyalty: If you're a long-time customer, emphasize your loyalty and inquire about loyalty discounts or promotions.

Choose the Right Time:

Renewal Periods: Negotiate around renewal periods or when contracts are up for renewal. Service providers are often more willing to make concessions to retain customers.

Contact Customer Service:

Be Polite and Courteous: Approach customer service representatives with politeness and courtesy. A courteous and upbeat tone can make a big difference. Express Your Concerns: Clearly articulate your concerns, emphasizing that you're looking for ways to reduce costs without compromising quality.

Be Prepared to Walk Away:

Alternative Options: Have a backup plan or explore alternative service providers. Being prepared to walk away gives you leverage in negotiations.

Bundle Services for Discounts:

Combine Services: Inquire about package deals or bundle services for potential discounts. Companies often provide better rates for customers who use multiple services.

Highlight Competitor Offers:

Mention Competitor Deals: Politely mention competitive offers or promotions you've come across. This signals to the service provider that you are actively exploring alternatives.

Negotiate Fees and Charges:

Request Fee Waivers: If you incur fees, such as late payment fees or service charges, ask for them to be waived. A polite and positive tone can have a significant impact.

Use Loyalty or Referral Programs:

Loyalty Rewards: Inquire about loyalty programs or referral incentives. Companies may offer discounts or additional benefits to customers who refer new clients.

Seek Senior or Loyalty Discounts:

Inquire About Senior Discounts: If applicable, inquire about senior discounts. Some service providers offer reduced rates for older customers.

Loyalty Discounts: Ask about loyalty discounts, especially if you've been a consistent and long-term customer.

Be Patient and Persistent:

Persistence Pays Off: If the initial response is not favorable, be patient and persistent. Ask to speak with a supervisor or explore other avenues for negotiation.

Get Agreement in Writing:

Confirm in Writing: Once you reach an agreement, ensure that the new terms are documented in writing. This protects both parties and avoids misunderstandings in the future.

Review Regularly:

Regular Check-Ins: Make it a habit to review your bills and services regularly. Market conditions and promotions change, and you may find new opportunities for negotiation.

Express Willingness to Refer:

Offer Positive Feedback: Express your satisfaction with the service and your willingness to recommend the company positively. This may motivate them to offer better terms.

Tips for Successful Negotiations:

Stay Calm and Collected: Maintain a calm and collected demeanor throughout the negotiation process.

Be Well-Informed: Knowledge about competitors' offers and market rates gives you a stronger negotiating position.

Build Rapport: Establishing a positive rapport with customer service representatives can enhance your chances of a successful negotiation.

By adopting a proactive and strategic approach to negotiating bills and services, you can unlock opportunities for savings and potentially improve the value you receive from essential services. Remember, the key is to be respectful, well-informed, and persistent in seeking the best possible terms for your financial well-being.

Avoiding Impulse Purchases

Impulse purchases can quickly derail your budget and financial goals. Learning to curb spontaneous buying habits is a valuable skill that contributes to better financial health. Here are practical strategies to help you avoid impulse purchases and make more intentional spending decisions:

Create a Budget:

Set Spending Limits: Establish clear spending limits for different categories in your budget. This offers a structure for prudent financial management.

Identify Triggers:

Emotional Triggers: Recognize emotional triggers that lead to impulse buying. Stress, boredom, or excitement can influence impulsive behavior.

Make a Shopping List:

Plan Ahead: Before shopping, create a detailed list of items you genuinely need. Follow the list to prevent making needless purchases.

Implement the 24-Hour Rule:

Delay Purchases: When tempted to make an impulse buy, wait 24 hours before making a decision. This cooling-off period helps you assess the necessity of the purchase.

Set Financial Goals:

Define Objectives: Establish short-term and long-term financial goals. Keeping these goals in mind can deter impulsive spending that hinders progress.

Use Cash Instead of Cards:

Physical Money: Pay with cash whenever possible. Observing actual cash disappear from your wallet may increase your awareness of your expenditures.

Unsubscribe from Retail Emails:

Reduce Temptation: Minimize exposure to sales and promotions by unsubscribing from retail newsletters. This reduces the temptation to make unplanned purchases.

Avoid Window Shopping:

Stay Focused: If you're prone to impulse buying, avoid browsing stores without a specific purpose. Window shopping can lead to unplanned purchases.

Shop with a Purpose:

Mission-Focused Shopping: Enter stores with a clear purpose and specific items in mind. Avoid meandering through aisles without intent.

Track Your Spending:

Maintain Records: Regularly track your expenses to identify patterns of impulsive spending. Awareness is the first step to change.

Ask Yourself Questions:

Assess Necessity: Before making a purchase, ask yourself if it's a need or a want. Assessing the necessity helps filter out impulsive buys.

Consider the Opportunity Cost:

Evaluate Alternatives: Think about the opportunity cost of the impulse purchase. What other meaningful ways could that money be used?

Set Spending Rules:

Establish Guidelines: Define rules for yourself, such as limiting the number of impulse purchases per month or setting a maximum dollar amount.

Practice Mindfulness:

Be Present: Practice mindfulness when shopping. Stay present and conscious of your actions to avoid falling into autopilot spending.

Enlist an Accountability Partner:

Seek Support: Share your goal of avoiding impulse purchases with a friend or family member who can help keep you accountable.

Unfollow Influencers or Brands:

Social Media Detox: If social media contributes to impulsive buying, unfollow influencers or brands that promote excessive consumerism.

Focus on Quality Over Quantity:

Invest Wisely: Prioritize quality over quantity. Investing in durable, high-quality items may cost more initially but can save money in the long run.

Practice Gratitude:

Appreciate What You Have: Cultivate a mindset of gratitude. Reflect on the things you already own, reducing the desire for unnecessary acquisitions.

Reward Yourself Mindfully:

Celebrate Achievements: When achieving financial milestones, celebrate mindfully. Choose rewards that align with your goals rather than indulging in impulse purchases.

Educate Yourself on Consumer Psychology:

Understand Marketing Tactics: Learn about marketing techniques designed to trigger impulse buying. Being aware of these tactics empowers you to resist them.

Tips for Success:

Start Small: Gradually incorporate these strategies into your routine to avoid feeling overwhelmed.

Celebrate Progress: Acknowledge and celebrate small victories in curbing impulsive spending.

Reflect Regularly: Periodically assess your spending habits and adjust strategies as needed.

By adopting these mindful spending practices, you can break the cycle of impulse buying and make more intentional choices that align with your financial goals. Remember, the key is to be conscious, deliberate, and disciplined in your approach to spending.

Cost-Cutting Tips For Common Expenses

Effectively managing common expenses is a key component of maintaining a healthy financial outlook. By implementing smart cost-cutting strategies, you can optimize your spending and allocate more funds towards your savings or other financial goals. Here are practical tips to cut costs in various common expense categories:

Housing Costs:

Refinance Your Mortgage: Explore refinancing options to secure a lower interest rate on your mortgage, potentially reducing monthly payments.

Rent Negotiation: If renting, inquire about the possibility of reducing rent, especially if you've been a long-term tenant.

Utilities:

Energy Efficiency: Implement energy-saving practices at home, such as using energy-efficient appliances and turning off lights and electronics when not in use.

Shop Around for Providers: Regularly compare utility providers to ensure you're getting the best rates on services like electricity, gas, and internet.

Groceries:

Meal Planning: Plan your meals for the week and create a shopping list to avoid unnecessary purchases.

Buy in Bulk: To save money, buy non-perishable goods in large quantities.

Use Coupons and Cashback Apps: Leverage coupons and cashback apps to get discounts on your grocery purchases.

Transportation:

Carpooling and Ridesharing: Share rides with colleagues or friends to split transportation costs.

Public Transportation: If possible, use public transportation to save on fuel and parking expenses.

Regular Vehicle Maintenance: Maintain your car regularly to prevent costly repairs and improve fuel efficiency.

Insurance:

Shop Around for Quotes: Periodically obtain quotes from different insurance providers to ensure you're getting the best rates.

Bundle Insurance Policies: Consider bundling your home and auto insurance policies with the same provider for potential discounts.

Debt Payments:

Refinance High-Interest Debt: Explore options to refinance high-interest loans or credit card debt to lower interest rates.

Consolidate Loans: Consolidate multiple loans into a single, more manageable payment.

Dining Out:

Cook at Home: Reduce the frequency of dining out by cooking at home. This not only saves money but is often healthier.

Lunch Prepping: Bring your lunch to work instead of buying it every day.

Entertainment Subscriptions:

Evaluate Necessity: Assess your entertainment subscriptions and consider canceling those you rarely use.

Share Subscriptions: Share subscription costs with family or friends to split expenses.

Cell Phone Plans:

Review Data Usage: Regularly review your data usage and adjust your plan accordingly to avoid ove*rpaying.*

Explore Budget-Friendly Plans: Research and switch to budget-friendly cell phone plans that meet your needs.

Credit Card Fees:

Avoid Late Fees: Pay credit card bills on time to avoid late fees.

Negotiate Interest Rates: Contact your credit card company to negotiate lower interest rates.

Health and Wellness:

Generic Medications: Opt for generic versions of medications to save on prescription costs.

Preventive Care: Prioritize preventive care to avoid more significant healthcare costs down the line.

Education Expenses:

Explore Financial Aid: Investigate financial aid options and scholarships for education expenses.

Used Textbooks: Consider buying used textbooks or exploring digital versions to cut down on textbook costs.

Personal Care and Beauty:

DIY Beauty Treatments: Experiment with at-home beauty treatments instead of frequenting salons.

Discounted Products: Purchase personal care and beauty products during sales or with discounts.

Subscription Services:

Cancel Unused Subscriptions: Regularly review your subscription services and cancel those you no longer use.

Share Accounts: Share subscription accounts with family or friends to split costs.

Home Repairs and Maintenance:

DIY Fixes: Learn to handle basic home repairs and maintenance tasks to save on professional service costs.

Preventive Maintenance: Regularly perform preventive maintenance to avoid costly repairs.

Clothing and Accessories:

Shop Secondhand: Explore thrift stores or online platforms for secondhand clothing and accessories.

Wait for Sales: Be patient and wait for sales or clearance events before making clothing purchases.

Fitness Memberships:

At-Home Workouts: Explore free or low-cost workout options at home to avoid expensive gym memberships.

Community Classes: Participate in community fitness classes or activities that may be more budget-friendly.

Pet Expenses:

Buy in Bulk: Purchase pet supplies in bulk to save on costs.

Regular Vet Checkups: Prioritize regular veterinary checkups to prevent costly health issues.

Technology and Electronics:

Limit Upgrades: Avoid unnecessary technology upgrades and only invest when truly necessary.

Refurbished Electronics: Consider purchasing refurbished electronics for cost savings.

Bank Fees:

Choose No-Fee Accounts: Select bank accounts that offer minimal or no fees.

ATM Usage: Use in-network ATMs to avoid additional fees.

Tips for Successful Cost Cutting:

Regular Review: Periodically review your budget and expenses to identify additional areas for cost-cutting.

Negotiate Bills: Don't hesitate to negotiate bills, including utilities, insurance, and subscription services.

Set Savings Goals: Allocate the money saved from cost-cutting to specific savings goals.

By implementing these cost-cutting tips, you can optimize your spending habits, reduce unnecessary expenses, and make your budget work more effectively for your financial well-being. Remember, the key is to be proactive, mindful, and open to exploring alternatives that align with your financial goals.

Chapter 4: Managing Debt Payment

Good debt vs. Bad debt

Understanding the distinction between good debt and bad debt is crucial for making informed financial decisions. While debt is often viewed negatively, not all debts are created equal. Here's a breakdown of the concepts of good debt and bad debt to help you navigate the financial landscape:

Good Debt:

Mortgage Debt:

Purpose: Taking on a mortgage to buy a home is generally considered good debt.

Reasoning: Real estate has the potential to appreciate over time, making homeownership an investment. Mortgage interest may also be tax-deductible.

Student Loan Debt:

Purpose: Borrowing for education to enhance career prospects is often seen as good debt.

Reasoning: Education can increase earning potential, leading to a positive return on investment. Student loan interest may also be tax-deductible.

Business Loans:

Purpose: Borrowing to start or expand a business is generally considered good debt.

Reasoning: A well-executed business venture can generate income and contribute to overall financial growth.

Investment Loans:

Purpose: Borrowing for investments, such as real estate or stocks, can be seen as good debt.

Reasoning: If the returns on the investments exceed the cost of the debt, it can lead to wealth accumulation.

Car Loans (in Some Cases):

Purpose: Financing a reliable and necessary vehicle may be considered good debt.

Reasoning: A reliable vehicle can enhance work opportunities and daily life, contributing to overall financial stability.

Bad Debt:

Credit Card Debt:

Purpose: Accumulating high-interest debt through credit cards for non-essential purchases is often considered bad debt.

Reasoning: High-interest rates can lead to substantial financial burdens, and the purchases may not contribute to long-term financial well-being.

Consumer Loans:

Purpose: Borrowing for non-essential items like luxury goods or vacations is generally considered bad debt.

Reasoning: These loans often have high-interest rates and may not provide long-term value or generate income.

Payday Loans:

Purpose: Short-term loans with extremely high-interest rates are widely regarded as bad debt.

Reasoning: The high cost of borrowing and potential for a debt cycle make payday loans financially detrimental.

High-Interest Personal Loans:

Purpose: Borrowing at high interest rates for discretionary spending may be considered bad debt.

Reasoning: The high cost of interest can outweigh the benefits of the purchases made with the loan.

Auto Loans for Depreciating Assets:

Purpose: Financing a vehicle that rapidly depreciates in value can be seen as bad debt.

Reasoning: The vehicle's value declines over time, potentially leaving you with a loan balance higher than the car's worth.

Key Considerations:

Interest Rates:

Good Debt: Typically comes with lower interest rates, making the cost of borrowing more manageable.

Bad Debt: Often associated with high-interest rates, leading to higher overall repayment amounts.

Potential Return on Investment:

Good Debt: Has the potential to generate returns or enhance your financial situation over time.

Bad Debt: Does not contribute to wealth-building or financial stability.

Necessity and Purpose:

Good Debt: Often incurred for essential purposes or investments with long-term benefits.

Bad Debt: Tends to be associated with non-essential, discretionary spending.

Financial Impact:

Good Debt: Generally contributes positively to your overall financial health.

__Bad Debt:__ Can lead to financial stress, especially when interest accumulates.

Tips for Managing Debt:

__Prioritize High-Interest Debt__: Focus on paying off high-interest debts first to minimize overall interest payments.

__Create a Repayment Plan:__ Establish a realistic plan to pay down debts systematically.

__Emergency Fund:__ Build an emergency fund to help cover unexpected expenses without resorting to high-interest debt.

__Financial Education:__ Stay informed about personal finance to make sound decisions about borrowing and debt management.

In summary, good debt is typically associated with investments that can enhance your financial well-being over time, while bad debt often involves high-interest borrowing for non-essential or depreciating assets. It's essential to assess the purpose, interest rates, and potential long-term impact of any debt before deciding whether it falls into the category of good or bad debt.

Strategies For Paying Off Credit Cards Quickly

Paying off credit card debt quickly is a commendable goal that can significantly improve your financial well-being. High-interest rates on credit cards can lead to financial stress, but with strategic planning and discipline, you can become debt-free. Here are effective strategies to expedite the process:

Create a Comprehensive Budget:

Income vs. Expenses: Outline your monthly income and expenses to understand where your money is going.

Identify Areas to Cut: Pinpoint discretionary spending and non-essential expenses that can be redirected towards debt repayment.

Prioritize High-Interest Debts:

List Outstanding Balances: Create a list of all your credit card debts, including outstanding balances and interest rates.

Tackle High-Interest Debt First: Focus on paying off the card with the highest interest rate first to minimize overall interest payments.

Implement the Debt Snowball Method:

Order Debts by Balance: Arrange debts from smallest to largest balance, regardless of interest rates.

Build Momentum: Pay off the smallest balance first, then use those payments to tackle the next smallest debt. This creates a momentum of success.

Consolidate Debt with a Balance Transfer:

Transfer to Low or 0% APR Card: Consider transferring high-interest balances to a card with a lower or 0% introductory APR.

Note Transfer Fees: Be mindful of transfer fees and the duration of the introductory APR period.

Negotiate Lower Interest Rates:

Contact Creditors: Reach out to your credit card companies and negotiate lower interest rates.

Highlight Good Payment History: Emphasize your commitment to repayment and your history as a responsible borrower.

Generate Extra Income:

Part-Time Work or Side Hustle: Explore opportunities for part-time work or side hustles to generate additional income.

Allocate Extra Earnings: Direct any extra income specifically towards credit card debt repayment.

Sell Unnecessary Items:

Declutter: Sell items you no longer need or use to generate extra cash.

Apply Sales to Debt: Direct the proceeds from sales towards your credit card debt.

Use Windfalls Wisely:

Tax Refunds or Bonuses: Apply unexpected windfalls, such as tax refunds or work bonuses, towards credit card debt.

Avoid Splurging: Resist the temptation to splurge on non-essential purchases with windfall money.

Cut Monthly Expenses:

Review Subscriptions: Cancel or downgrade subscription services to free up additional funds.

Limit Dining Out: Reduce discretionary spending on dining out and entertainment.

Automate Payments:

Set Up Auto-Payments: Automate minimum payments to ensure you never miss a due date.

Supplement with Manual Payments: Make additional manual payments whenever possible to accelerate debt reduction.

Snowflake Payments:

Apply Windfalls Immediately: Use any unexpected small sums of money immediately to make extra payments.

Round Up Payments: Round up your monthly payments to the nearest ten or twenty dollars.

Seek Professional Advice:

Credit Counseling: Consider seeking advice from a reputable credit counseling agency.

Debt Management Plans: Explore debt management plans that may help negotiate lower interest rates and consolidated payments.

Stay Motivated:

Celebrate Milestones: Celebrate small victories along the way to staying motivated.

Visualize Debt-Free Future: Imagine the financial freedom and reduced stress that comes with being debt-free.

Educate Yourself on Personal Finance:

Understand Credit Card Terms: Familiarize yourself with credit card terms, interest rates, and payment structures.

Improve Financial Literacy: Educate yourself on personal finance to make informed decisions about spending and debt management.

Seek Support:

Accountability Partner: Share your goal of paying off credit card debt with a friend or family member who can provide support and accountability.

Financial Forums: Join online forums or communities where individuals share their debt payoff journeys for inspiration.

Avoid Accumulating New Debt:

Use Cash or Debit: Consider using cash or debit for purchases to avoid accumulating new credit card debt.

Emergency Fund: Create an emergency fund to help you pay for unforeseen costs and lessen your reliance on credit.

Review Progress Regularly:

Monitor Debt Reduction: Regularly assess your progress and adjust strategies as needed.

Celebrate Successes: Acknowledge milestones and successes in your journey to becoming debt-free.

By combining these strategies and staying disciplined, you can expedite the process of paying off credit card debt and regain control of your financial future. The key is to be proactive, focused, and persistent in your efforts to achieve financial freedom.

Consolidating Payments And Loans

Consolidating payments and loans is a strategic financial move that can simplify your financial life and potentially save you money. This process involves combining multiple debts or payments into a single, more manageable payment. Whether it's credit cards, student loans, or other types of debt, consolidation can offer various benefits. Here's a comprehensive guide to help you understand and navigate the process:

Understanding Debt Consolidation:

Debt Consolidation Loans:

Purpose: A debt consolidation loan involves taking out a new loan to pay off multiple existing debts.

Advantages: Offers the convenience of a single monthly payment and, if the new loan has a lower interest rate, can lead to reduced overall interest payments.

Balance Transfer Credit Cards:

Purpose: Transferring high-interest credit card balances to a new card with a lower or 0% introductory APR.

Advantages: Can provide a temporary interest-free period, allowing you to pay down the principal more quickly.

Home Equity Loans or Lines of Credit:

Purpose: Using the equity in your home to secure a loan for debt consolidation.

Advantages: May offer lower interest rates, and the interest may be tax-deductible, but it puts your home at risk if you're unable to repay.

Student Loan Consolidation:

Purpose: Combining multiple federal student loans into a single loan with a fixed interest rate.

Advantages: Simplifies repayment and may extend the repayment term, reducing monthly payments.

Benefits of Consolidating Payments and Loans:

Simplified Finances:

Single Monthly Payment: Instead of juggling multiple payments, consolidation provides the convenience of one monthly payment.

Lower Interest Rates:

Reduced Overall Interest: If the new loan or credit card has a lower interest rate, you may save money on interest payments over time.

Fixed Interest Rates:

Stability: Many consolidation loans offer fixed interest rates, providing stability and predictability in payments.

Extended Repayment Terms:

Lower Monthly Payments: Extending the repayment term can lead to lower monthly payments, making it more manageable for your budget.

Improved Credit Score:

Timely Payments: With simplified payments, you're more likely to make timely payments, positively impacting your credit score.

Potential for Debt Payoff:

Faster Repayment: With lower interest rates or extended terms, you may be able to pay off your debt more quickly.

Considerations Before Consolidating:

Overall Debt Load:

Assess Total Debt: Understand the total amount of debt you have before considering consolidation.

Interest Rates:

Compare Rates: Compare the interest rates of your existing debts with the rates offered by consolidation options.

Fees and Costs:

Evaluate Fees: Be aware of any fees associated with consolidation, such as loan origination fees or balance transfer fees.

Credit Score:

Impact on Credit: While consolidating can positively impact your credit in the long run, the initial application may result in a temporary dip.

Financial Discipline:

Avoid New Debt: Consolidation is most effective when you commit to not accumulating new debt.

Budgeting:

Create a Budget: Develop a realistic budget to ensure you can comfortably afford the consolidated payment.

Step-by-Step Guide to Debt Consolidation

List Your Debts:

Catalog Existing Debts: Create a comprehensive list of all your debts, including balances and interest rates.

Explore Consolidation Options:

Research Loan Options: Investigate different consolidation loans, credit cards, or programs tailored to your specific debts.

Check Your Credit Score:

Credit Report Review: Obtain your credit report to ensure accuracy and understand your creditworthiness.

Calculate Savings and Costs:

Estimate Savings: Calculate potential savings by comparing the total cost of existing debts with the consolidated option.

Factor in Fees: Consider any fees associated with the consolidation process.

Apply for the Consolidation Option:

Submit Applications: Apply for the chosen consolidation option, ensuring you meet the eligibility criteria.

Review Terms and Conditions:

Understand Agreements: Thoroughly review the terms and conditions of the consolidation loan or credit card.

Consolidate and Repay:

Use Funds Appropriately: If approved, use the funds to pay off existing debts promptly.

Commit to Repayment: Stick to the agreed-upon repayment plan and avoid accumulating new debt.

Monitor Your Finances:

Regular Check-Ins: Periodically review your budget and financial goals to ensure you remain on track.

Tips for Successful Debt Consolidation:

Seek Professional Advice: Consult with financial advisors or credit counselors for personalized guidance.

Negotiate Rates: Don't hesitate to negotiate interest rates or fees with lenders to secure more favorable terms.

Emergency Fund: Build and maintain an emergency fund to avoid reliance on credit in case of unexpected expenses.

Debt consolidation can be a powerful tool for simplifying your finances and accelerating your journey to financial stability. However, it's essential to approach it thoughtfully, considering your unique financial situation and goals. By making informed decisions and staying disciplined, you can use consolidation to regain control of your financial future.

Handling Student Loans And Mortgages

Handling Student Loans and Mortgages: Navigating Your Financial Responsibilities

Managing student loans and mortgages is a significant aspect of financial planning for many individuals. Both of these financial obligations play a crucial role in shaping your long-term financial well-being. Here's a comprehensive guide on how to effectively handle and navigate student loans and mortgages:

Understand Your Student Loans: *Know the Terms:* Be familiar with the terms of your student loans, including interest rates, repayment options, and any grace periods.

Create a Repayment Plan:

Evaluate Repayment Options: Understand various repayment plans, such as standard, income-driven, or graduated plans.

Set a Budget: Create a budget that allows for consistent monthly payments towards your student loans.

Prioritize High-Interest Loans:

Target High-Interest Debts: If you have multiple student loans, prioritize paying off those with higher interest rates first to save on overall interest costs.

Explore Loan Forgiveness Programs:

Public Service Loan Forgiveness: Determine if you qualify for public service loan forgiveness if you work in a qualifying public service job.

Consolidate or Refinance:

Consolidation: Consider federal loan consolidation for a simplified repayment process.

Refinance: Explore private loan refinancing for potentially lower interest rates, but be aware of losing federal loan benefits.

Stay Informed About Deferment or Forbearance Options:

Temporary Relief: Understand the options for deferment or forbearance if you face temporary financial challenges.

Automate Payments:

Set Up Auto-Pay: Automate your student loan payments to ensure they are consistently paid on time.

Budget for Student Loan Payments:

Include in Monthly Budget: Make student loan payments a non-negotiable part of your monthly budget.

Mortgages:

Understand Your Mortgage Terms:

Know the Details: Familiarize yourself with the terms of your mortgage, including interest rates, loan duration, and any prepayment penalties.

Make Timely Payments:

Avoid Late Payments: Ensure that you make your mortgage payments on time to maintain a positive credit history.

Explore Refinancing:

Lower Interest Rates: Consider refinancing your mortgage if interest rates have significantly decreased since you obtained your loan.

Shorten Loan Term: Explore the option of refinancing to a shorter loan term to pay off your mortgage more quickly.

Create an Emergency Fund:

Prepare for Unexpected Expenses: Build and maintain an emergency fund to cover unexpected expenses and avoid financial strain on mortgage payments.

Accelerate Mortgage Payments:

Extra Payments: If possible, make additional payments towards your mortgage principal to reduce the overall interest paid and shorten the loan term.

Monitor Housing Market Conditions:

Stay Informed: Keep an eye on housing market conditions, as changes may impact the value of your property.

Consider Home Equity Options:

Home Equity Loans or Lines of Credit: Explore home equity options cautiously, considering the impact on your overall financial stability.

Review Homeowner's Insurance:

Regular Assessments: Periodically review and update your homeowner's insurance coverage to ensure it adequately protects your investment.

Plan for Property Taxes:

Include in Budget: Incorporate property taxes into your budget, setting aside funds in escrow if required by your mortgage agreement.

Prepare for Home Maintenance Costs:

Set Aside Funds: Plan for routine maintenance and repairs by setting aside funds in your budget.

Evaluate Mortgage Assistance Programs:

Explore Options: Research and explore mortgage assistance programs that may provide relief during financial hardships.

Be Mindful of Home Equity:

Use Wisely: If considering a home equity loan, use the funds judiciously for essential purposes rather than non-essential spending.

Understand the Risks of Adjustable-Rate Mortgages (ARMs):

Anticipate Rate Changes: If you have an ARM, understand the potential for interest rate fluctuations and plan accordingly.

Review and Update Wills and Beneficiaries:

Estate Planning: Regularly review and update your will and beneficiaries to reflect any changes in your financial situation or family structure.

Professional Financial Advice:

Consult Financial Advisors: Seek advice from financial professionals to ensure your mortgage aligns with your long-term financial goals.

Communicate with Lenders:

If facing financial challenges, communicate with your lenders early. Many mortgage lenders have hardship programs that can offer temporary relief.

Reevaluate Homeownership Goals:

Adjust Plans if Necessary: Regularly reassess your homeownership goals and whether they align with your overall financial objectives.

Be Mindful of Home Equity Conversion Mortgages (HECMs):

Understand Reverse Mortgages: If considering a reverse mortgage, known as a Home Equity Conversion Mortgage (HECM), understand the terms and potential implications.

Review and Compare Insurance Policies:

Shop Around for Rates: Periodically review and compare homeowner's insurance rates to ensure you are getting the best coverage for the cost.

Build Home Equity Wisely:

Home Improvements: Consider strategic home improvements that can increase the value of your property over time.

Financial Planning for Paying Off Mortgage:

Create a Payoff Plan: If feasible, create a plan for paying off your mortgage early to reduce interest payments.

Be Cautious About Taking on Additional Debt:

Avoid Unnecessary Loans: Be cautious about taking on additional debt, especially if it could impact your ability to meet mortgage obligations.

Stay Informed About Market Trends:

Interest Rate Monitoring: Keep an eye on market trends, especially interest rates, to make informed decisions about your mortgage.

Utilize Windfalls Wisely:

Consider Paying Down Mortgage: If you receive unexpected financial windfalls, consider using a portion to make extra mortgage payments.

Reassess Financial Goals Periodically:

Adjust According to Life Changes: Periodically reassess your overall financial goals, adjusting them as needed to align with changes in your life or financial situation.

Seek Professional Advice When Needed:

Consult with Financial Advisors: If you have complex financial concerns related to your mortgage, seek guidance from financial advisors or mortgage professionals.

Keep an Eye on Interest Rate Trends:

Potential Refinancing Opportunities: Monitor interest rate trends and seize opportunities to refinance if it aligns with your financial goals.

Save for Future Homeownership Expenses:

Plan for Property Taxes and Insurance: Set aside funds regularly to cover property taxes and insurance, ensuring you are financially prepared for these ongoing expenses.

Be Aware of Mortgage Scams:

Stay Informed: Be vigilant against mortgage scams and fraudulent activities, especially if you're exploring refinancing or loan modifications.

Focus on Overall Financial Health:

Holistic Approach: Consider your mortgage as part of your broader financial health. Prioritize building a well-rounded financial foundation.

Handling student loans and mortgages requires a balanced approach that considers both short-term financial goals and long-term financial well-being. Regularly review and reassess your financial situation, staying informed about market trends, and seek professional advice when needed. By managing these financial responsibilities wisely, you can achieve greater financial stability and work towards your broader financial objectives.

Maintaining Good Credit Scores

Your credit score is a crucial component of your financial well-being, influencing your ability to secure loans, obtain favorable interest rates, and even impact job opportunities. Maintaining a good credit score requires diligence, responsible financial habits, and strategic planning. Here's a comprehensive guide on how to maintain and improve your credit score:

Understanding Credit Scores:

What is a Credit Score?

A credit score is a numerical representation of your creditworthiness, typically ranging from 300 to 850. Higher scores indicate lower credit risk.

Factors Affecting Credit Scores:

Payment History (35%): Timely payments on credit accounts.

Credit Utilization (30%): The ratio of credit used to credit available.

Length of Credit History (15%): How long your accounts have been active.

Types of Credit in Use (10%): The variety of credit accounts you have.

New Credit (10%): Recent applications for credit.

Strategies for Maintaining Good Credit Scores:

Regularly Check Your Credit Report:

Review Annually: Obtain free credit reports annually from each of the major credit bureaus (Equifax, Experian, TransUnion) to check for errors or unauthorized activities.

Timely Payments are Non-Negotiable:

Set Up Auto-Pay: Automate payments to ensure bills are paid on time. Payment history is a significant factor in your credit score.

Manage Credit Utilization:

Keep Balances Low: Aim to keep credit card balances below 30% of your credit limit to demonstrate responsible credit usage.

Avoid Closing Old Credit Accounts:

Length of Credit History Matters: Closing older accounts can shorten your credit history, potentially impacting your credit score.

Diversify Your Credit Portfolio:

Have a Mix of Credit: A healthy mix of credit types, such as credit cards, installment loans, and retail accounts, can positively influence your credit score.

Limit New Credit Applications:

Apply Strategically: Limit the number of new credit applications, especially within a short period, as multiple inquiries can temporarily lower your score.

Communicate with Lenders During Financial Hardship:

Negotiate with Creditors: If facing financial challenges, communicate with creditors to explore options rather than missing payments.

Educate Yourself on Credit Management:

Understand Credit Terms: Familiarize yourself with terms like APR, interest rates, and credit limits to make informed credit decisions.

Tips for Credit Score Improvement:

Address Outstanding Debts:

Prioritize Repayment: Focus on paying down existing debts to reduce credit utilization and improve your credit score.

Seek Professional Advice:

Credit Counseling: Consider seeking guidance from a reputable credit counseling agency to develop a tailored plan for credit improvement.

Negotiate with Creditors:

Discuss Settlements: If struggling with debt, negotiate with creditors for settlements or revised payment plans.

Credit-Building Tools:

Secured Credit Cards: Consider using secured credit cards to rebuild credit. These require a cash deposit and often have lower approval requirements.

Become an Authorized User:

Leverage Someone Else's Good Credit: Being added as an authorized user on an account with a positive payment history can positively impact your credit.

Dispute Inaccuracies:

Regularly Check Reports: Dispute inaccuracies promptly with credit bureaus to ensure your credit report accurately reflects your financial history.

Be Patient:

Credit Score Improvement Takes Time: Positive changes in credit behavior take time to reflect in your credit score. Be patient and consistent in your efforts.

Credit Score Maintenance for Different Life Stages:

Young Adults:

Start Building Credit Early: Open a credit account, such as a student credit card, to begin establishing a credit history.

New Homebuyers:

Maintain Stability: Keep financial stability during the homebuying process by avoiding major credit changes or new debts.

Parents:

Educate Children About Credit: Instill good financial habits in your children, teaching them about responsible credit use.

Retirees:

Monitor for Identity Theft: Retirees are often targeted for identity theft. Regularly monitor your credit for any suspicious activities.

Common Credit Score Myths:

Checking Your Own Credit Hurts Your Score:

Myth: Checking your own credit (soft inquiry) does not impact your score. Only hard inquiries from potential lenders affect it.

Closing Credit Cards Boosts Your Score:

Myth: Closing credit cards can shorten your credit history and potentially harm your credit score.

High Income Means Higher Credit Score:

Myth: Your income is not directly considered in your credit score. Creditors assess your ability to manage debt, not your income.

Bankruptcy Ruins Your Credit Forever:

Myth: While bankruptcy has a significant impact, credit can be rebuilt over time with responsible financial behavior.

Always Carrying a Balance Helps Your Score:

Myth: Carrying a balance doesn't improve your credit. Timely payments and low credit utilization are more critical.

Maintaining good credit scores is a continuous process that involves responsible financial habits, regular monitoring, and strategic decision-making. By understanding the factors that influence your credit score and adopting proactive credit management strategies, you can build and sustain a healthy credit profile over time.

Chapter 5: Growing Your Savings

Setting Up Emergency Fund

An emergency fund is a financial cushion that provides peace of mind and protection against unexpected expenses or income disruptions. Establishing this safety net is a fundamental step toward financial stability. Here's a comprehensive guide on how to set up and manage an emergency fund:

Understanding the Importance of an Emergency Fund:

Financial Security:

Safety Net: An emergency fund serves as a safety net, ensuring you have funds readily available for unexpected expenses.

Reduced Stress: Having a financial buffer reduces stress and allows you to navigate unexpected challenges with greater ease.

Avoiding Debt:

Preventing Debt Accumulation: An emergency fund helps you avoid accumulating debt when faced with sudden expenses, eliminating the need for high-interest loans or credit cards.

Financial Flexibility:

Flexibility in Decision-Making: With an emergency fund, you can make financial decisions based on your long-term goals rather than reacting to immediate financial crises.

Job Loss or Income Interruptions:

Income Protection: In case of job loss or income interruptions, an emergency fund provides a financial cushion until you can secure alternative income sources.

Determining Your Emergency Fund Goal:

Calculate Monthly Expenses:

List Essential Costs: Make a list of your essential monthly expenses, including rent or mortgage, utilities, groceries, insurance, and debt payments.

Assess Personal Risk Factors:

Evaluate Job Stability: Consider the stability of your job or income source. Individuals with less job security may need a larger emergency fund.

Healthcare Considerations: Evaluate factors like health conditions that may impact your need for emergency funds.

Set Realistic Goals:

Start Small: If needed, start with a small initial goal and gradually work towards building a more robust emergency fund.

Follow General Guidelines:

3 to 6 Months' Worth: Aim to save at least three to six months' worth of living expenses. Some individuals may need a more substantial fund based on their circumstances.

Creating Your Emergency Fund:

Choose a Dedicated Account:

Separate from Regular Accounts: Open a separate savings account specifically designated for your emergency fund to avoid accidental spending.

Automate Contributions:

Set Up Automatic Transfers: Schedule automatic transfers from your primary checking account to your emergency fund. Consistency is key to steady growth.

Allocate Windfalls:

Use Unexpected Income Wisely: Direct unexpected windfalls, such as tax refunds or work bonuses, towards your emergency fund.

Cut Non-Essential Expenses:

Review Budget: Identify non-essential expenses and redirect those funds towards your emergency fund. Sacrifices now contribute to financial security later.

Side Hustles or Part-Time Work:

Explore Additional Income: Consider taking on side hustles or part-time work to supplement your income specifically for building the emergency fund.

Set Milestones:

Celebrate Achievements: Break your goal into milestones and celebrate when you reach each one. It keeps you motivated and helps track your progress.

Managing and Maintaining Your Emergency Fund:

Periodic Reviews:

Adjust as Needed: Periodically review your emergency fund goal, especially after significant life changes like job changes, marriage, or the birth of a child.

Replenish After Withdrawals:

Prioritize Refill: If you need to dip into your emergency fund, make replenishing it a priority to maintain its effectiveness.

Explore High-Interest Savings Accounts:

Maximize Earnings: Consider placing your emergency fund in a high-interest savings account to maximize its growth while keeping it easily accessible.

Educate Family Members:

Family Awareness: Ensure that family members are aware of the purpose of the emergency fund and discourage unnecessary withdrawals.

Emergency Fund, Not Investment:

Low-Risk Approach: The primary purpose of an emergency fund is liquidity and accessibility, not high returns. Keep it in low-risk, easily accessible accounts.

Financial Education:

Understand Fund Usage: Educate yourself and family members on when it's appropriate to use the emergency fund to avoid unnecessary withdrawals.

Regularly Reevaluate Expenses:

Adjust Budget: As your life circumstances change, regularly reassess your budget to ensure your emergency fund aligns with your current needs.

Can I Use Investments for My Emergency Fund?

While investments can provide higher returns, an emergency fund should be easily accessible. Consider maintaining a separate investment portfolio for long-term goals.

Should I Include Debt Payments in My Monthly Expenses?

If your debt payments are essential monthly expenses, include them in your calculation. However, the ultimate goal is to eliminate debt so that your emergency fund covers necessary living expenses.

What Constitutes an Emergency?

Emergencies are unexpected, urgent, and necessary expenses, such as medical bills, car repairs, or sudden job loss. They are not for planned expenses or discretionary spending.

Is Three to Six Months' Worth of Expenses a Fixed Rule?

The three to six months' guideline is a general recommendation. Individuals with more unpredictable circumstances may consider saving a more substantial emergency fund.

Can I Adjust My Emergency Fund Goal Over Time?

Absolutely. Life circumstances change, and your emergency fund goal should reflect these changes. Regularly reassess and adjust your goal as needed.

Setting up and maintaining an emergency fund is a foundational element of sound financial planning. By being proactive, consistent, and adaptable to changing circumstances, you can build a financial safety net that provides security and flexibility in the face of life's uncertainties.

Taking Advantage Of Employer Retirement Plans

Taking Advantage of Employer Retirement Plans: Building a Financial Foundation

Employer-sponsored retirement plans are valuable tools for securing your financial future, offering tax advantages and a structured way to save for retirement. Understanding and maximizing these benefits can significantly enhance your long-term financial well-being. Here's a comprehensive guide on how to take full advantage of employer retirement plans:

Types of Employer Retirement Plans:

401(k) Plans:

Employee Contributions: Employees can contribute a portion of their pre-tax income to a 401(k) account, with contributions subject to annual limits set by the IRS.

Employer Matching: Some employers offer matching contributions, enhancing the overall contribution to the employee's retirement savings.

403(b) Plans:

Nonprofit and Educational Institutions: Similar to a 401(k), a 403(b) plan is designed for employees of nonprofit organizations and educational institutions.

457 Plans:

Governmental Employees: Available for employees of state and local governments, as well as certain nonprofit organizations, a 457 plan allows contributions on a pre-tax or Roth basis.

IRA-Based Plans:

Simplified Employee Pension (SEP) IRA: Employers contribute to traditional IRAs on behalf of employees.

Simple IRA: Suited for small businesses, allowing both employer and employee contributions.

Key Advantages of Employer Retirement Plans:

Tax Benefits:

Pre-Tax Contributions: Contributions to traditional 401(k) and similar plans are made with pre-tax dollars, reducing your taxable income.

Tax-Deferred Growth: Earnings within the plan grow tax-deferred until withdrawal in retirement.

Employer Matching Contributions:

Free Money: Employer matching contributions are essentially free money. Take full advantage by contributing enough to capture the entire employer match.

Automatic Payroll Deductions:

Consistent Contributions: Employer retirement plans typically allow for automatic payroll deductions, ensuring consistent contributions without manual effort.

Investment Options:

Diverse Investment Choices: Plans offer a range of investment options, allowing you to tailor your portfolio based on risk tolerance and financial goals.

Creditor Protection:

Legal Safeguards: Retirement accounts often have protections against creditors, providing an added layer of security.

Contribute Enough to Receive Full Employer Match:

Maximize Matching Contributions: Contribute at least enough to receive the full employer match. It's a crucial step in maximizing your retirement savings.

Take Advantage of Catch-Up Contributions:

Age 50 and Older: Individuals aged 50 and older can make additional catch-up contributions beyond the standard limits.

Understand Vesting Schedules:

Vesting Periods: Be aware of vesting schedules for employer contributions. Ensure you understand when you are entitled to the full value of employer matches.

Diversify Your Investments:

Balanced Portfolio: Diversify your investments within the plan to manage risk and optimize returns. Consider your risk tolerance and time horizon.

Regularly Review and Adjust Contributions:

Budget for Increases: As your income grows, increase your contributions to employer retirement plans. Regularly review and adjust your contributions as needed.

Consider Roth Options:

Roth 401(k) or Roth 403(b): If available, consider contributing to a Roth option within your employer plan for tax-free withdrawals in retirement.

Avoid Early Withdrawals:

Penalties and Taxes: Avoid early withdrawals, as they may be subject to penalties and taxes. Employer retirement plans are designed for long-term savings.

Stay Informed About Plan Changes:

Communicate with HR: Stay informed about any changes to the employer retirement plan. Regularly communicate with the HR department to understand updates.

Retirement Planning Beyond Employer Plans:

Individual Retirement Accounts (IRAs):

Supplemental Savings: Consider opening and contributing to an IRA for additional retirement savings.

Financial Education:

Continuous Learning: Stay informed about retirement planning strategies, investment options, and changes in tax laws. Continuous learning is key to making informed decisions.

Professional Financial Advice:

Consult Financial Advisors: Seek guidance from financial advisors to create a comprehensive retirement plan aligned with your goals.

Coordinate with Other Investments:

Holistic Approach: Coordinate employer retirement plans with other investment accounts to create a holistic retirement strategy.

Emergency Fund and Debt Management:

Financial Stability: Maintain an emergency fund and manage debts effectively to ensure financial stability both before and during retirement.

Employer-sponsored retirement plans are powerful tools for building financial security in retirement. By understanding the specific features of your plan, maximizing contributions, and staying informed about retirement planning strategies, you can make the most of these opportunities and set the stage for a comfortable and secure retirement.

Investing Strategies - Stocks, Mutual Funds

Investing is a powerful tool for wealth creation, and understanding different strategies is crucial for making informed decisions. Two popular investment options are individual stocks and mutual funds. Here's a comprehensive guide on investing strategies for both:

Investing in Individual Stocks:

Research and Due Diligence:

Company Analysis: Thoroughly research individual companies before investing. Analyze financial statements, industry trends, and the company's competitive position.

Diversification:

Spread Risk: Diversify your stock portfolio across various sectors and industries to reduce risk. Avoid overconcentration in a single stock.

Long-Term Perspective:

Patience Pays Off: Investing in individual stocks often requires a long-term perspective. Be patient and avoid making impulsive decisions based on short-term market fluctuations.

Dividend Investing:

Regular Income: Consider stocks with a history of paying dividends. Dividend investing provides a regular income stream and can contribute to long-term wealth.

Value Investing:

Buy Undervalued Stocks: Follow a value investing approach by seeking stocks that are undervalued compared to their intrinsic value.

Growth Investing:

Focus on Growth Potential: Look for companies with strong growth potential. These stocks may have higher volatility but can offer significant returns over time.

Stay Informed:

Continuous Learning: Stay informed about market trends, economic indicators, and any news that might impact the companies in your portfolio.

Utilize Fundamental and Technical Analysis:

Fundamental Metrics: Assess fundamental metrics like earnings, revenue growth, and debt levels.

Technical Analysis: Consider using technical analysis to identify entry and exit points based on historical price patterns.

Set Realistic Goals:

Define Objectives: Clearly define your investment goals and risk tolerance. Adjust your portfolio strategy accordingly.

Regularly Review and Rebalance:

Adjust Portfolio: Periodically review your stock portfolio, rebalancing it to align with your investment goals and market conditions.

Investing in Mutual Funds:

Understand Fund Types:

Equity Funds: Invest in stocks and aim for capital appreciation.

Bond Funds: Focus on fixed-income securities, providing regular interest payments.

Index Funds: Mimic a specific market index's performance.

Sector Funds: Concentrate on specific industries or sectors.

Diversification Through Mutual Funds:

Built-In Diversification: Mutual funds inherently offer diversification by holding a variety of securities. This reduces risk compared to investing in individual stocks.

Professional Management:

Expertise at Work: Mutual funds are managed by professional fund managers who make investment decisions on behalf of investors.

Low Entry Barrier:

Accessible to Small Investors: Mutual funds allow small investors to access a diversified portfolio with a relatively low initial investment.

Automatic Investment Plans:

Systematic Investment: Many mutual funds offer systematic investment plans (SIPs), allowing investors to contribute fixed amounts regularly.

Choose Based on Goals:

Match Fund Objectives: Select mutual funds based on your investment goals, risk tolerance, and time horizon.

Expense Ratio Consideration:

Cost Analysis: Be aware of the fund's expense ratio, which represents the cost of managing the fund. Lower expense ratios are generally preferable.

Performance Track Record:

Historical Performance: Evaluate a mutual fund's historical performance, keeping in mind that past performance is not a guarantee of future results.

Regular Monitoring:

Stay Informed: Although managed by professionals, regularly monitor the performance of your mutual funds to ensure they align with your objectives.

Asset Allocation with Mutual Funds:

Blend Different Types: Use different types of mutual funds for a well-rounded asset allocation strategy that aligns with your risk tolerance and financial goals.

Common Principles for Both Stocks and Mutual Funds:

Risk Management:

Assess Risk Tolerance: Understand your risk tolerance and invest accordingly. Diversification is a key strategy for managing risk.

Long-Term Focus:

Patience and Discipline: Both stock and mutual fund investing benefit from a long-term perspective. Avoid making impulsive decisions based on short-term market movements.

Regular Review and Adjustments:

Adapt to Changes: Periodically review your investment portfolio, making adjustments as needed based on changes in your financial situation, goals, and market conditions.

Stay Informed:

Continuous Learning: Markets evolve, and staying informed about economic trends, financial news, and investment strategies is crucial for making informed decisions.

Diversification:

Spread Out Investments: Diversify your investments to mitigate risk. A well-diversified portfolio can help navigate market volatility.

Set Realistic Goals:

Define Objectives: Clearly define your investment goals, whether it's retirement, education, or wealth creation. Align your investment strategy with these objectives.

Consider Professional Advice:

Financial Advisors: Consult with financial advisors to receive personalized guidance based on your unique financial situation and goals.

Be Mindful of Fees:

Cost Analysis: Whether investing in stocks or mutual funds, be mindful of fees and expenses. Minimizing costs contributes to overall investment returns.

Investing in individual stocks and mutual funds offers unique opportunities and challenges. By understanding your financial goals, risk tolerance, and time horizon, you can develop a well-rounded investment strategy that aligns with your aspirations for financial success. Whether you choose to invest in individual stocks, mutual funds, or a combination of both, the key is to stay informed, stay disciplined, and adapt your strategy as needed over time.

Saving For Large Purchases

Saving for Large Purchases: A Strategic Guide

Saving for significant expenses, whether it's a home, a car, education, or a dream vacation, requires thoughtful planning and disciplined financial habits. Here's a comprehensive guide to help you save effectively for large purchases:

Define Your Goal:

Be Specific: Clearly define the purpose of your savings. Knowing the exact amount and timeframe will guide your savings strategy.

Create a Budget:

Track Your Finances: Develop a comprehensive budget that outlines your income, expenses, and savings goals. Identify areas where you can cut back to allocate more towards saving.

Open a Dedicated Savings Account:

Separate Funds: Open a separate savings account specifically for your large purchase goal. This separation makes it easier to track progress and prevents accidental spending.

Set Realistic Milestones:

Break Down the Goal: Divide your overall savings goal into smaller, achievable milestones. Celebrate each milestone to stay motivated.

Automate Your Savings:

Set Up Automatic Transfers: Schedule automatic transfers from your primary checking account to your dedicated savings account. This ensures consistent contributions.

Prioritize Your Savings:

Treat It as a Non-Negotiable Expense: Consider your savings as a non-negotiable monthly expense. Prioritize it alongside essential bills.

Cut Unnecessary Expenses:

Identify Non-Essentials: Analyze your spending habits and cut back on non-essential expenses. Redirect these funds towards your savings goal.

Earn Extra Income:

Side Hustles or Freelancing: Explore opportunities to earn extra income through side hustles or freelancing. Direct these earnings towards your savings.

Take Advantage of Windfalls:

Tax Refunds, Bonuses, or Gifts: Allocate unexpected windfalls, such as tax refunds or work bonuses, towards your savings goal.

Explore High-Interest Savings Accounts:

Maximize Returns: Consider placing your savings in high-interest savings accounts to earn more on your money while keeping it easily accessible.

Review and Adjust:

Regularly Assess Your Budget: Periodically review your budget and adjust your savings plan based on changes in income, expenses, or your overall financial situation.

Consider Investment Options:

Longer Time Horizon Goals: If your large purchase is several years away, explore investment options like mutual funds or bonds for potentially higher returns.

Be Patient and Persistent:

Stay Committed: Saving for significant purchases requires patience. Stay committed to your plan, even during challenging financial periods.

Avoid Debt for the Purchase:

Discipline in Financing: Whenever possible, avoid using debt to fund your large purchase. Save up in advance to maintain financial discipline.

Comparison Shop:

Find the Best Deals: When your goal is nearing fruition, comparison shop for the best deals. This ensures you get the most value for your money.

Negotiate:

Don't Hesitate to Bargain: Whether it's a car or a home, don't hesitate to negotiate. You might secure a better price or favorable financing terms.

Reevaluate Along the Way:

__Adjust for Changing Circumstances:__ Life circumstances can change. Periodically reassess your savings goals and adjust your strategy if needed.

Learn About Financing Options:

__Understand Loan Options:__ If you decide to finance part of the purchase, understand the available loan options and choose the one that aligns with your financial goals.

Celebrate Achievements:

__Acknowledge Your Progress:__ Celebrate each milestone and the ultimate achievement of reaching your savings goal. It reinforces positive financial habits.

Build a Contingency Fund:

__Account for Unforeseen Expenses:__ Alongside your savings, build a contingency fund to cover unforeseen expenses related to your large purchase.

Seek Professional Guidance:

__Financial Advisors:__ If you're unsure about the best approach, consult with a financial advisor for personalized guidance tailored to your specific situation.

Saving for large purchases requires discipline, planning, and commitment. By setting realistic goals, creating a dedicated savings plan, and staying focused on your budget, you can work towards achieving your financial aspirations. Whether it's a home, car, education, or a dream vacation, strategic saving brings you closer to turning those dreams into reality.

Automating Your Savings

Automating your savings is a powerful financial strategy that ensures consistent contributions toward your financial goals without the need for constant manual intervention. Whether you're saving for emergencies, a home, retirement, or other objectives, automating the process simplifies your financial journey. Here's a comprehensive guide on how to automate your savings effectively:

Set Clear Financial Goals:

Define Objectives: Clearly outline your financial goals, whether it's an emergency fund, a down payment for a house, or retirement savings. Knowing your objectives helps determine the amount you need to save.

Create a Budget:

Understand Your Finances: Develop a comprehensive budget that includes your income, fixed expenses, discretionary spending, and savings goals. A budget provides a roadmap for your financial decisions.

Identify Monthly Savings Targets:

Break Down Goals: Break down your savings goals into monthly targets. This step makes it easier to determine how much to automate each month.

Open Dedicated Savings Accounts:

Separate Goals: Open separate savings accounts for different financial goals. This separation helps you track progress and prevents mingling of funds.

Set Up Automatic Transfers:

Utilize Online Banking: Most banks offer online platforms that allow you to schedule automatic transfers between accounts. Set up recurring transfers to move money from your checking to your savings accounts.

Align Transfers with Paydays:

Match Income Timing: Schedule transfers to coincide with your payday. This ensures that savings are prioritized before discretionary spending.

Utilize Employer Payroll Systems:

Direct Deposit Options: If your employer offers direct deposit, allocate a portion of your paycheck to be directly deposited into your savings account.

Explore Employer Retirement Plans:

Automatic 401(k) Contributions: Contribute to employer-sponsored retirement plans, such as a

401(k), through automatic payroll deductions. It's a convenient way to save for the future.

Implement Automatic Investment Plans:

Investing Automatically: If you're saving for long-term goals, consider automatic investment plans for mutual funds or exchange-traded funds (ETFs). This ensures consistent investment contributions.

Use Savings Apps:

Fintech Solutions: Explore savings apps and fintech solutions that offer features like round-up transactions or automatic savings transfers. These apps can streamline the process.

Set Reminders for Reviews:

Regularly Assess Progress: Set reminders to review your savings goals periodically. Adjust your automated transfers if your financial situation or goals change.

Increase Contributions with Pay Raises:

Leverage Income Increases: Whenever you receive a salary increase or bonus, consider increasing your automated savings contributions. It's a painless way to boost savings.

Consistency is Key:

Build Habitual Behavior: Automating savings cultivates a consistent saving habit. Over time, this behavior becomes ingrained, making it easier to meet financial goals.

Emergency Fund First:

Prioritize Liquidity: If you're just starting, prioritize building an emergency fund. Automate contributions to this fund before focusing on other goals to ensure financial stability.

Explore Automatic Debt Repayment:

Automatic Loan Payments: If you have outstanding debts, set up automatic payments to ensure timely repayments. This helps avoid late fees and boosts your credit score.

Leverage Bonuses or Windfalls:

Direct Unexpected Funds to Savings: Whenever you receive unexpected funds, such as tax refunds or work bonuses, consider directing a portion to your savings goals.

Educate Yourself on Automation Tools:

Stay Informed: Stay informed about new automation tools and features offered by banks and financial institutions. These innovations can enhance your savings strategy.

Adjust for Life Changes:

Adapt to Circumstances: Life circumstances change. Be prepared to adjust your automated savings plan when you experience significant life events like marriage, childbirth, or job changes.

Monitor for Fraud:

Regularly Check Accounts: Regularly review your accounts for any unauthorized transactions or suspicious activities. Automated transfers should be monitored to ensure accuracy.

Seek Professional Guidance:

Financial Advisors: Consult with financial advisors to tailor your automated savings plan based on your unique financial situation and goals.

Automating your savings is a practical and efficient way to achieve financial goals. By leveraging technology, you can build wealth consistently without the stress of manual transfers. Whether you're saving for short-term needs or long-term objectives like retirement, automating your savings ensures that financial progress remains on track, even in the midst of a busy life.

CONCLUSION

Recap of Key Takeaways

Navigating the realm of budgeting and financial management can be empowering, setting the stage for a secure and prosperous future. Let's recap the key takeaways from our exploration of how to budget and manage money wisely:

Introduction:

Acknowledged the prevalence of financial struggles due to poor money management.

Introduced the guide as a solution to readers' money woes.

Overview of the Importance of Budgeting:

Emphasized that budgeting is a foundational aspect of financial health.

Discussed how a well-structured budget provides clarity and control over one's finances.

The Benefits of Effective Money Management:

Explored the positive impact of effective money management on reducing stress and achieving financial goals.

Highlighted the importance of building an emergency fund for unexpected expenses.

Short-Term, Mid-Term, and Long-Term Goals:

Defined and differentiated between short-term, mid-term, and long-term financial goals.

Emphasized the need to align budgeting and saving strategies with specific goals.

Planning for Expenses vs. Wants:

Discussed the importance of distinguishing between necessary expenses and discretionary spending.

Advised prioritizing needs over wants when creating a budget.

Lifestyle Factors to Consider:

Explored how lifestyle choices impact financial decisions.

Encouraged readers to align their spending habits with their values and long-term goals.

Importance of Goal Setting:

Discussed the significance of setting clear and achievable financial goals.

Emphasized that goals provide direction and motivation for effective money management.

Types of Budgets (Zero-Based, 50/30/20, etc.):

Introduced various budgeting approaches, including zero-based budgeting and the 50/30/20 rule.

Advised readers to choose a budgeting method that suits their financial situation and goals.

Calculating Income and Expenses:

Discussed the importance of accurately calculating both income and expenses.

Highlighted the need for a comprehensive understanding of one's financial inflows and outflows.

Recommended Budget Percentages:

Provided general guidelines on budget percentages for categories like housing, transportation, and savings.

Emphasized the flexibility to adjust percentages based on individual circumstances.

Sample Budgets for Different Incomes:

Offered sample budgets for various income levels to provide practical insights.

Demonstrated that effective budgeting is possible regardless of income level.

Budgeting Tools and Apps:

Introduced the role of technology in simplifying budgeting with the use of tools and apps.

Encouraged readers to leverage these resources for greater financial control.

Big Expense Areas to Cut Back On:

Identified common areas where individuals can cut back on expenses.

Encouraged a critical evaluation of spending habits for potential savings.

Finding Little Ways to Save Daily:

Explored practical tips for saving money in daily life, such as packing lunch or using public transportation.

Highlighted the cumulative impact of small, consistent savings.

Negotiating Bills and Services:

Encouraged readers to negotiate bills and services for potential savings.

Provided tips on how to approach negotiations effectively.

Avoiding Impulse Purchases:

Discussed the pitfalls of impulse purchases and their impact on a budget.

Advised adopting strategies like creating shopping lists and avoiding emotional buying.

Cost-Cutting Tips for Common Expenses:

Shared cost-cutting tips for common expenses, such as utilities and groceries.

Stressed the importance of being mindful and seeking value in spending.

Good Debt vs. Bad Debt:

Differentiated between good and bad debt, emphasizing the potential benefits of strategic borrowing.

Encouraged readers to manage debts responsibly and prioritize paying off high-interest debt.

Strategies for Paying Off Credit Cards Quickly:

Discussed effective strategies for paying off credit card debt, including the snowball and avalanche methods.

Emphasized the importance of consistent payments.

Consolidating Payments and Loans:

Explored the option of consolidating multiple debts for simplification and potential cost savings.

Advised careful consideration of the terms and impact on overall finances.

Handling Student Loans and Mortgages:

Discussed strategies for managing student loans and mortgages effectively.

Encouraged seeking options like income-driven repayment plans for student loans.

Setting Up Emergency Fund:

Emphasized the critical role of an emergency fund in financial stability.

Advised building an emergency fund gradually for sound financial planning.

Maintaining Good Credit Scores:

Explored the components of credit scores and their significance.

Provided strategies for maintaining and improving credit scores over time.

Taking Advantage of Employer Retirement Plans:

Highlighted the benefits of employer-sponsored retirement plans and the importance of maximizing contributions.

Advised leveraging automatic payroll deductions for consistent savings.

Investing Strategies - Stocks, Mutual Funds:

Explored strategies for investing in individual stocks and mutual funds.

Emphasized the need for diversification, understanding risk tolerance, and aligning investments with financial goals.

Saving for Large Purchases:

Discussed strategic approaches to saving for significant expenses, including setting clear goals and creating a dedicated savings plan.

Advised prioritizing savings and avoiding unnecessary debt.

Automating Your Savings:

Explored the benefits of automating savings for consistency and convenience.

Provided practical tips for setting up automatic transfers and leveraging technology for financial automation.

In conclusion, mastering the art of budgeting and financial management involves a combination of discipline, knowledge, and strategic planning. By incorporating these key takeaways into your financial habits, you can build a solid foundation for a secure and prosperous future. Remember, financial success is a journey, and each step toward better money management contributes to long-term well-being.

Encouragement for Continued Financial Success

Embarking on the journey toward financial success is an empowering endeavor that requires dedication, resilience, and a commitment to ongoing improvement. As you navigate the path of managing your money wisely, here's a heartfelt encouragement to inspire and sustain your pursuit of continued financial success:

Celebrate Your Achievements:

Take a moment to acknowledge and celebrate every financial milestone, no matter how small. Each step forward is a triumph and a testament to your commitment.

Embrace the Learning Process:

Financial education is a lifelong journey. Embrace the learning process, stay curious, and continuously seek knowledge about personal finance to make informed decisions.

Adapt to Change:

Life is dynamic, and so are your financial circumstances. Be adaptable and open to adjusting your strategies as life evolves. Flexibility is a key component of sustained financial success.

Prioritize Financial Well-Being:

Place a high value on your financial health. Recognize that managing your money wisely is a crucial aspect of overall well-being and security for you and your loved ones.

Stay Consistent with Good Habits:

Consistency is the backbone of financial success. Maintain good habits, whether it's sticking to a budget, saving regularly, or making informed investment choices.

Surround Yourself with Positivity:

Cultivate a positive financial environment. Seek support from friends, family, or financial communities that share your values and encourage responsible financial behavior.

Set New Goals:

As you achieve your initial financial goals, set new ones to keep the momentum going. Setting and pursuing new objectives helps you stay motivated and engaged in your financial journey.

Celebrate Progress, Not Perfection:

Financial success is about progress, not perfection. Understand that setbacks may occur, but what matters most is your commitment to learning from them and moving forward.

Build Resilience:

Financial challenges are a part of life. Build resilience to overcome setbacks, learn from experiences, and use adversity as a stepping stone toward greater financial strength.

Practice Gratitude:

Cultivate gratitude for the resources and opportunities you have. A grateful mindset fosters contentment and can positively impact your financial decisions.

Seek Professional Guidance:

Don't hesitate to consult with financial advisors or experts when needed. Their guidance can provide valuable insights and help you make informed decisions aligned with your goals.

Encourage Others:

Share your financial journey with others and encourage them to embark on their path to financial success. Helping others creates a positive ripple effect in your community.

Enjoy the Journey:

Financial success is not just about reaching the destination; it's about the journey. Enjoy the process of learning, growing, and achieving your financial aspirations.

Focus on What You Can Control:

Some aspects of the financial landscape may be beyond your control. Focus on what you can control—your spending habits, savings, and investment decisions.

Visualize Your Future:

Envision the financial future you desire. Having a clear picture of your goals can serve as a powerful motivator and guide your actions.

Practice Self-Compassion:

Be kind to yourself. Financial success involves a series of choices, and not every decision will be perfect. Learn from mistakes, but also practice self-compassion along the way.

Embrace the Freedom of Financial Security:

Visualize the freedom that comes with financial security. It offers the flexibility to pursue your passions, support loved ones, and contribute to causes that matter to you.

Stay Mindful of Your Values:

Align your financial decisions with your values. A mindful approach to money ensures that your choices reflect what truly matters to you.

Savor the Accomplishments:

Take a moment to savor the accomplishments along your financial journey. Whether it's paying off debt, reaching a savings goal, or investing wisely, relish the sense of achievement.

Believe in Your Potential:

You have the power to shape your financial destiny. Believe in your potential to create a secure and prosperous future through wise financial management.

Remember, the journey to financial success is a marathon, not a sprint. Each decision you make today contributes to your financial well-being tomorrow. By staying committed, remaining adaptable, and celebrating your progress, you are nurturing the foundation for a future filled with financial success and peace of mind. Your dedication is the key to unlocking the doors of financial opportunity and fulfillment. Keep moving forward with confidence and determination—your financial success story is still unfolding.